Welcome to the
ancient Chinese path
of Fo Ling,

Avani —

☆ ☆

DRIVING

OWN

Swami

Beyondananda's

YOUR KARMA
Tour Guide to Enlightenment

BY

SWAMI BEYONDANANDA

WITH STEVE BHAERMAN

DESTINY BOOKS
Rochester, Vermont

Destiny Books
One Park Street
Rochester, Vermont 05767

Library of Congress Cataloging-in-Publication Data

Beyondananda, Swami.
Driving your own Karma.

1. Enlightenment (Buddhism)—Humor.   2. Karma—Humor.
I. Bhaerman, Steve.   II. Title.
PN6231.E63B49   1989   818'.5402   89-16769
ISBN 0-89281-253-2

Printed and bound in the United States.

3   5   7   9   10   8   6   4   2

Destiny Books is a division of Inner Traditions International, Ltd.

Distributed to the book trade in the United States by Harper and Row
Publishers, Inc.

Distributed to the book trade in Canada by Book Center, Inc., Montreal,
Quebec

Contents

Acknowledgments

I'd like to acknowledge the following people for their assistance, knowing or unknowing, in writing this book:

My parents and family for encouraging and nurturing my sense of humor.

My childhood dentist, Dr. Max Mitchell, who through his friendship and outrageous sense of humor showed me that life could be fun after all.

Mad Magazine, Groucho Marx, H. Allen Smith, and Lenny Bruce.

Larry Kelsaw, co-creator of my first humorous publication, States Wire Service, who helped me respect my skills as a humorist and experience the powerful ability of laughter to change behavior.

Josh Pokempner, co-writer of Swami in the early days, whose own sense of humor, zaniness, and wisdom helped shape Swami's character.

Allan Barsky, who suggested that I turn Swami into a stand-up comedy act.

Arnold Patent, who insisted for years that I should be doing nothing but comedy.

Don McMillan, who helped me learn the practical skills to make my dream a reality.

Joel Goldstein, who doggedly pursued me to record a Swami album, and who has been Swami's most loyal and vocal spokesman.

Ed and Gail Tossing—Gail for her faith in the book project, Ed for his co-creation of Swami's rap song, both for their friendship.

Jan Stabler, who invested in the book project before he even met me, and who did whatever was necessary to get Swami on the road—and out to the masses—in a brand new van and trailer.

Paula, Nance, Leslie, Kurt and Anne, Emmy, Paul and Charles, and Curtis and Jeanine for sharing their homes and work spaces so I could write this book while on the road.

Our friends in Ann Arbor, Santa Cruz, and across the country too humorous to mention whose faith and support helped us along the way.

My wonderful editor, Leslie Colket, who was appropriately firm and flexible in helping shape this book.

Artist Michael Abey for his rendition of the cover, and art director Estella Arias for her thoroughness and patience in working with an author who was always on the road.

And most of all, my beautiful wife Trudy, who got to experience a lot more of my Scorpio than my Libra while this book was being written.

☆

AFTERWORD
How to Survive the Coming Good Years: Swami Beyondananda's Message from the Future

Editor's note: In an attempt to insure that this book is absolutely ahead of its time, we decided to begin with an interview conducted with Swami Beyondananda after one of his recent trips to the future. Although he usually eschews making predictions, we offered him great sums of money and Swami reluctantly gave in to the prophet motive.

US: *We couldn't help but notice that you're a little late for this interview. Any explanations?*

SWAMI: Actually, I was on one of my trips to the future and I was having so much fun, I lost track of time. It was very exciting indeed. I was at the 1998 World Series. Now I don't want to spoil it for your readers by telling you who won, but I will say this. The Moscow Proletarians haven't had a good left-handed relief pitcher since they moved the franchise from Cleveland.

US: *I'm sure our readers are all curious. How, actually, do you travel into the future?*

SWAMI: It is all done with the mind. You just have to think ahead.

US: *And how do you return?*

SWAMI: You just think back.

US: *Can you be a little more specific?*

SWAMI: Well, the first thing to remember is that we are not our bodies. I know many of you will be relieved to hear this. So the first step is to close your eyes, and take off your body. That's right, just zip it down the front. Some of you ladies have the zipper in back, so you might need some help. Good. Now step out of your body and look at it just sitting there. I must tell you the first time I did this and sat down next to my body, I was beside myself with excitement.

US: *It's really that easy to travel out of your body?*

SWAMI: Oh, it is. It's great traveling without your body because you don't have to pack any clothes, you never have to worry about finding a bathroom, and there's never a problem with getting bumped off of an astral flight. And it's all nonsmoking. But there *are* two important things to remember when traveling out of your body. The first is, when you leave your body always leave it running. This is very important. The second is, never lock your keys inside. You will look very foolish trying to break into your body with a coathanger.

US: *That seems like very wise advice. How long do these astral flights take, Swami?*

SWAMI: Well, since everything is happening simultaneously on the astral plane, it takes no time at all.

US: *What's it like in these timeless astral states?*

SWAMI: For one thing, you never hear anyone say, "See you later." Since everyone is always here right now, there's not a lot of privacy. I tried taking my body on an astral trip one time, and I said never again. Imagine trying to eat, sleep, go to the bathroom, watch a ballgame, make love, meditate, and have an intelligent conversation all at the same time. Forget it! That's why when we're in bodies, we create the illusion of time. Time is indeed an illusion, but don't try telling that to your boss when you're forty-five minutes late.

US: *Swami, you seem to be traveling in the future a lot these days. I thought the best place to be in is the now.*

SWAMI: Oh, I'm in the now when I travel to the future. Only it's a later now. It's very difficult to think and be in the now at the same time. As soon as you think, "Aha, *now* I'm in the now," it's already later, and your now is a then. So I don't bother trying to live in the now, because it's impossible. As a matter of fact, living in the present is a thing of the past. After all, the present is here today and gone tomorrow while the future is always ahead. So I say, we might as well learn to live in the future, because we're going to be there sooner or later.

In the future, time travel will be commonplace. People will not only vacation in the future, but they will visit the past as well—just for old time's sake. In fact, these will be some *real* time-share vacations. You'll see classified ads like, "Lovely English cottage to share for the summer of 1645," or "Condo on Mars, 2068, half-price during asteroid season." You take a vacation in prehistoric times, I guarantee you'll have no trouble getting folks to sit through your vacation slides. The only problem will be explaining to Jimmy why he can't take the stegosaurus eggs home to hatch for his science project.

US: *That's amazing. What else can you tell us about the future? What about those predicted earth changes? Are they going to happen?*

SWAMI: Yes, there will be powerful changes on the planet indeed. As you know, technocrats have been practicing unnatural forms of earth control for many years now, and these have had many damaging side effects, including infertility. In the future, food growers and energy harvesters will switch to the old-fashioned rhythm method—being in harmony with Mother Earth's own rhythms.

US: *How will these changes come about?*

SWAMI: Well, as you know, Earth has been a kind and patient mother with her impetuous children. Even though we're always trampling her garden and fighting with our brothers and sisters, she never nags or yells, "Wait until your Father gets home!" But given all the toxic chemicals we humans are trashing the planet with, I can tell you Mother Earth is rapidly losing her sense of humus, and she certainly has no intention of getting her tubers tied. And when this Mother gets upset, look out! You or I might break out in acne if we have a toxic reaction. She breaks out in volcanoes.

US: *What about those violent upheavals predicted for California? Will they happen?*

SWAMI: Well, you know I hate to spoil the movie for people by telling them how it's going to turn out. Besides, Creative is still working on the script for that one. But I will say this. Unless there is a spiritual transformation, a lot of Californians are going to be converted to Quakers and Shakers.

US: *Speaking of the future, Swami, how will the world end?*

SWAMI: Like anything else. The music will fade, and they'll run the credits. But do not be concerned, my children. It is my understanding the Sponsor very much enjoys the show, and it should run for many, many more seasons.

US: *Another question I'm sure a lot of people are asking: Will the poles shift?*

SWAMI: Oh, yes. In fact, the Poles have already begun to shift, thanks to Lech Walesa. The Nigerians, the Mexicans, the Russians, the whole world will shift. It is inevitable. It is all part of Nonjudgment Day.

US: *So Nonjudgment Day is coming. How soon, Swami?*

SWAMI: Very soon. Indeed, the Harmonic Convergence was an important step in bringing about worldwide consciousness. Imagine hundreds of thousands of aware humans converging on the most powerful places on the planet with their harmonicas! This, by the way, is not to be confused with the *Phil*harmonic Convergence, which requires an entire orchestra.

US: *What exactly did the Harmonic Convergence accomplish?*

SWAMI: This event allowed each individual to truly become an instrument of peace. The resulting sound created a harmonic field around the planet that sounded to beings in nearby dimensions like the honking of a great horn, and they knew instantly that this signaled a major shift—our planetary karma had been shifted into surpassing gear.

You see, in the past most humans have believed that our karma drives us. But now we see that it is we who must drive our own karma. So the next phase of our education will be driver's education. No more will our religious leaders be able to say, "Leave the driving to us." No more automatic transmission. From now on, if we want to make a shift we must do it ourselves. And the acceleration in our evolution will be great.

US: *Nonjudgment Day—what will it be like?*

SWAMI: Well, imagine a world where no judgments are made! The Supreme Court will finally be able to throw away all those silly papers and do what they want to do—become a singing group. They will be called the Supremes, and Sandra Day O'Connor will give women a true voice in government. No more penalties will be called in football—the laws of karma will be sufficient. And we *all* will win beauty contests!

US: *That brings up an interesting question. What will happen to the military once Nonjudgment Day comes about? Will young people still have to go into the service?*

SWAMI: Oh, people will still go into the service, but this will be an entirely different kind of service. Young men and women who truly want to serve will go into the Pizza Corps, where they will deliver food to those in need. As waiters and waitresses, they will learn to serve others. In waiting, they will learn patience—and obedience as well, for every waiter must be able to take orders.

US: *You speak about delivering food to those in need. Right now hunger seems to be a major problem in the world. Will there still be hunger in the coming good years?*

SWAMI: Of course. Without hunger, how will people know when to eat? But there will be plenty of food and plenty of enjoyable work, so people will no longer have to sit passively in the "feed us" position waiting for a handout.

US: *What about all those government programs and social service agencies. What will they be doing?*

SWAMI: All government employees will have to take a Civil Circus Examination to help them figure out what is the most enjoyable way for them to serve. Some will become Comic-kazes and spread laughter and good cheer.

US: *And what about those who don't become Comic-kazes?*

SWAMI: Well, they can work with a group called Feels on Wheels and bring nurturing massage to those who are out of touch. Or if they are worried about rubbing people the wrong way, they can work with Oms for the Omless.

US: *Tell us about Oms for the Omless, Swami.*

SWAMI: Omlessness is one of the biggest problems we face. You see, so many people have learned to let religion or gurus determine their spiritual experience that they have forgotten how to attune themselves to the symphony of nature—and they don't feel at om. The Oms for the Omless program gives people a sound way to center themselves.

US: *And this will be for free?*

SWAMI: Oh, no. After all, money is a small price to pay for a mantra that will bring everlasting peace of mind. In fact, the program's motto is, "You pays your money and you takes your chants."

US: *Swami, earlier you mentioned "harvesting energy." That intrigued me. What forms of energy will we be using in the future?*

SWAMI: Well, it won't be oil and it won't be coal or gas—and it certainly won't be nuclear power. Remember back in the '70s when President Carter visited Three Mile Island and gave a glowing report? Well, he's still glowing! No, in the future we will become very much aware of energy fields that exist naturally. We will harvest these energy fields anytime we need to, for the supply is virtually endless. The actual process is too technical to go into right here, but suffice it to say we will be able to absorb energy from the cosmos through the process of cosmosis.

US: *You know, in all this talk of the new age you haven't said much about the traditional religions. What about these old standbys. How will they fare?*

SWAMI: Well, they will have to change with the times, to be sure. In keeping with the motif that accentuates the positive, the Catholics will be instituting "reverse confession," whereby you tell the priests everything you did *right* in the previous week. The Right-to-Lifers will still maintain that life begins at conception, but they will concede that it doesn't *end* at birth. Therefore, they will be putting most of their energy into caring for and feeding the world's children. And in the coming good years people will have saved themselves, so the televangelists will have to turn their attention to saving the whales instead. And that is a good thing, because it is a great human quality to work for something that is bigger than ourselves.

US: *Swami, you seem very optimistic about the future. Sure, you've been there to visit, but for the rest of us—what signs are there that things are indeed getting better?*

SWAMI: The signs are everywhere. Do you realize I've doubled last year's income and this year isn't half over yet? And I notice there's much less static lately when I meditate. Even my tennis game is improving.

US: *But that's just you. What about everyone else?*

SWAMI: No, no. Everyone's tennis game is getting better—I haven't won a match all year. Things are getting better and better all the time, and this is creating a terrible problem.

US: *I don't understand. What's so terrible about things getting better?*

SWAMI: Nothing, unless you've only prepared yourself for bad times. See, down through the ages people have always had reasons why they felt bad—it was the weather, or having to wait in the unemployment line, or the Republicans, or the Communists, or tired blood. Some people even blamed it on the Bossa Nova. Well, right now we're learning to solve our problems at an alarming rate. Now we must awaken to the ultimate problem: People think having it easy is going to be easy. But when you've been told things are tough, having it easy is really tougher than when things are tough.

US: *Huh?*

SWAMI: I'll explain further. You see, there's one thing that's easy when things are tough—and that's finding excuses for why things feel tough. But when things are easy and they still *feel* tough, explaining why they feel tough isn't easy. And believe me, that's tough.

US: *This interview isn't easy.*

SWAMI: That's tough.

US: *That's easy for you to say.*

SWAMI: That's right. But what I'm saying is, there's a way to have things feel easy even when they are tough. There are definitely some good years coming, but as the Karma Sutra tells us, if we want to be sure they come, we must stimulate them with the proper foreplay. Sure, out-of-body experiences can be a fun way to visit the future, but we need in-body experiences to make sure the kind of future we want is there when we get there. And the most important in-body experience we can have is joy. Any other questions?

US: *Swami, would you care to comment on the relationship between time and space?*

SWAMI: You know what? I think we are out of time.

US: *That's perfect, because we're out of space, too.*

☆
PART ONE
There's No Place
Like Om

AH, OM SWEET OM. You've heard of the sound of one hand clapping? The hum of the Universe after it's just had an attune up and is running just right has been compared to the sound of All Hands Clapping. And why not? The Universe is a pretty terrific show, although not without some flaws. No, it is not a bad piece of work when you consider that God created it for His seventh grade science project—and got a "C."

That wonderful sound, Om, is our hotline to Universal Intelligence and cosmic peace, but how soon we forget. We are like forever-hungry puppies, doggedly pursuing some elusive scent. Noses to the ground, our vision is narrowed as we focus on one detail after the other. Which of course doesn't work, because you can't have detail wagging the dog. And when our Master calls to tell us that He has pre-

9

pared our Gravy Train and it is waiting for us, we are too busy chasing rabbits to hear Him.

Sure, we want to be in charge of our lives, but life is a lot like football—if you want to be the Quarterback, you first have to know where your Center is. So in this section, I present a three-point plan for Om Improvement: 1) Eliminating Truth Decay; 2) Achieving Your Ideal Wait; and 3) Realizing that Nothing Is Important. Look at this section as a handbook for beginning your inward journey. Actually, it is more than a handbook, because it tells you what you can do with your whole body. And two more tips for exploring within: Be careful around the Islets of Langerhans, and please, my children, no sharp objects. So let's all relax, kick off our bodies, and head for Om.

HOW SWAMI LEARNED TO FEEL AT OM ANYWHERE

As a child growing up in Oklahoma, I never really felt at Om. Even as a youngster, I wanted to escape the restrictions of physical existence and fly to worlds unknown. I knew I was not my body, although I often wondered, "If I am not my body, then who is?" My dad, whose interest in the world of spirits was limited to what he could produce in his backyard still, tried to be understanding. He took me from spiritual master to spiritual master trying to get to the root of my restlessness. This was before the advent of MasterCard, so he had to pay cash for all of this.

I had many memorable teachers in those years. There was the Japanese master who taught the healing art of Joh-Rei (in Oklahoma they called it "Billy Joh-Rei"), the great guru of rock 'n' roll Baba Oom Mow Mow (his golden rule was, "Do wop unto others as you would have them do wop unto you"), and Red Baba, who taught the Western form of moving meditation called "T'ai Cobb." Yes, I mastered the forms of Pit Ching, Cat Ching, and Bun Ting and had dreams of going on to the highest form of all, Co Ching. But one day I had a transcendent experience while at the plate. Not only did I leave my body, but I left two runners in scoring position. The next day, Red Baba called me into his office to tell me I was about to experience T'ai Cobb's most transcendent form of all—unconditional release.

To help me with my concentration, my dad enrolled me in a concentration camp run by a Zen master named Yuan Tibet. And was I a difficult student! Whenever the master would come into the room, I would make irreverent comments or ask impertinent questions. He was quite patient with me for a week or two, but finally got tired of my baiting him. One day I was in the midst of one of my disruptive harangues and he quietly came over and rapped me smartly on the head with his stick. My head hurt for a week, but I had learned a lesson—master-baiting was bad for my health.

But my most memorable teacher of all was the great Native American shaman, Broken Wind. Not only did he teach me to converse with nature (without monopolizing the conversation like so many of us humans do) and take me on my first vision quest (a wilderness experience with an optometrist friend of his), but he finally put an end to my rebellious behavior. Because he was a roly-poly sort of fellow, I used to like to tackle him from behind and squeeze his stomach as hard as I could. I must say that he gently warned me several times not to do that, but I was too impetuous to listen. Finally, I did it once too often. True to his name, Broken Wind let go with an eruption that sent me sprawling across the room. I was a little surprised at this gut-level response to my provocation, but I had learned another valuable spiritual lesson: "Don't squeeze the shaman!"

It was Broken Wind who encouraged my levitation practice—he always said he enjoyed raising other people's kids—and told me that my levity would make it easier for me to meet my next great teacher. Soon after, I left Oklahoma and began to drift around the country. I often would hop freights, which isn't all that easy—some of those freights are twenty, thirty feet high. And I had many adventures. In Chicago, I met Swami Vitoananda, who taught me a simple three-word mantra which he said would always bring money—"Stick 'em up!" I sat in my room for weeks, uttering the mantra over and over again, but for some reason it didn't work and I left Chicago wondering if I would ever find my true teacher.

My next stop was New York, where I went through a time of constant questioning. I questioned myself so much I finally had to take the Fifth Amendment to get any peace. I had a succession of odd jobs in those days (being odd made me well-suited for this work), and I supplemented my meager income by doing baseball card readings—a skill I learned from the venerated Vietnamese umpire, Owen Thieu. (Thieu was a psychic as well, and he would infuriate pitchers and batters alike by calling the pitch before it was thrown.)

It was Thieu who told me I would meet my guru on a New Delhi pilgrimage. Since plane fare was out of the question, I figured I'd do the next best thing. Each week I made a pilgrimage to a new deli, hoping that the Universe wasn't a stickler for spelling. Then, one week it happened. I wandered into Louie's Finer Deli on Delancey Street and saw this luminescent being hovering at the top of the ceiling and blissfully munching a knish. With a heart full of joy and passion, I floated up to meet him. And that is how I met my beloved guru, Harry Cohen Baba, the Garment Center Saint—over lunch.

"Oh, great Arisen One," I began. "You are the teacher I have long been waiting for. I am here to serve you."

"Good," he said, "because the service in this place is lousy. Could you get me some mustard, and a cream soda please?"

When he had finished eating, he said, "So? What can I do for you?"

I told him I was searching for the Key to the Universe.

"Listen," he said, "I hate to tell you this, boychick, but there is no key to the Universe. That's the bad news. The good news is, it's been left unlocked."

"Unlocked?" I asked.

"Of course! Who's gonna steal? And besides, everyone knows that in a limitless Universe, there are no fences."

"Well," I said, "what I really mean is, I want to find myself. Can you help me?"

"I don't know," he said. "Where were you last time you looked? In my experience, you're always exactly where you put yourself."

And in that flash of enlightenment I realized that I was exactly where I had left me! "Oh, Master," I said blissfully. "I want to follow you wherever you go!"

"Okay," he shrugged. "But I tell you what. Do us both a favor and wait until I come out of the men's room, all right?"

The next several months were sheer bliss. The Garment Center Saint outfitted me with a brand new sutra and two pairs of chants. For the purpose of purification, he had me fast for forty days on Dr. Brown's Cel-Ray Soda. And yet, even in his ashram, even in the great teacher's presence, I still felt restless. Instead of the clear meditation I so fervently desired, I would often get static. One day, I asked my master, "Why all this interference with my meditation?"

And he related the following story:

THE GREAT SEPARATION

In the beginning, we were all One. Truly we were mirrors for each other. And this was good, especially for shaving. You could look at someone else and do a perfectly acceptable job. But even if you butchered your face and looked like you'd been pledging a German dueling fraternity, it was still okay. Everything was okay, since there was nothing to compare it to. In fact, there was one mood and one mood only—and that was ecstasy.

Now Adam—he wasn't really the first man, he just had the first press agent—was sitting around the garden one day blissfully watching the grass grow when a snake slithered up to him and said, "Hello there, Adam. How's it going?"

"Going?" Adam replied, puzzled. "It isn't going anywhere. It's all here now."

"No," said the snake. "I mean how are you feeling?"

"Feeling?" Adam asked. "Why, ecstatic. How else would I be feeling?"

"Everything is to your liking?" asked the snake.

"Sure. I get three squares a day, the sun in the morning and the moon at night, and a beautiful wife who doesn't spend a penny on clothes. What's not to like?"

"What did you have for breakfast?"

"Uh, let's see," said Adam. "A couple of figs, a pomegranate, some shellfish, a handful of grubs wrapped in some grape leaves—"

"Adam!" said the snake, shocked. "That's terrible! Don't you know anything about food combining?"

"Sure I do," said Adam. "I combine food all the time. I combine all kinds of food and I eat it and it tastes absolutely delicious."

"Grubs are delicious?" said the snake. "I'm a *snake* and I don't even eat grubs. They're disgusting!"

"Disgusting?" said Adam. "What does disgusting mean?"

"You know what the trouble with you is, Adam? You've got no judgment?"

"Judgment?"

"Yeah," said the snake, warming up to the subject. "Like that outfit you're wearing. Everyone knows flesh tones are out this year."

"Year?"

"Oh, brother," said the snake. "You don't know *anything*, do you? Listen, I have just the thing for you. It's called the Civilization Training, and for the small fee of 350 figs, we'll teach you everything you need to know to be successful in life. We'll even teach you meditation to help you get in touch with God."

"I don't understand," said Adam. "I'm already in touch with God. We're together all the time."

"Well, then," said the snake, "you need to develop some of your own interests. Get a little independent. Be in charge!"

"But why would I want to be in charge of my life when I'm provided with everything I want or need. And 350 figs? Why should I pick more than I can use?"

"You," said the snake disparagingly, "have the typical welfare mentality. You won't work, you won't save a thing, and not a thought for tomorrow. You're perfectly content to bask in the sun and smell the flowers while the Universe supports you. How long have you been here, anyway?"

"I dunno," shrugged Adam. "Seems like forever."

"Aha," said the snake. "That's because you're bored."

"Bored?"

"You need challenge in your life!"

"Challenge?"

"Yes, like a job."

"Job?"

"Yes, job. You'd make a terrific fig-picker."

"I am a terrific fig-picker—when I want figs."

"Would you pick figs for Eve?" asked the snake.

"For Eve? Sure, I'd pick some for her."

"Good," said the snake, "because she just finished the Civilization Training—and she owes me 350 figs."

And so Adam went to work picking figs, but it didn't end there.

Because as a result of the Civilization Training, Eve had gotten some ambition. She decided to be a fashion model, and let's face it—if you're going to be a fashion model you need clothes. And then Adam figured, what the heck, and he took the Civilization Training too. And before long, he'd built a luxurious home in the more fashionable section of Eden and then, of course, they had to have fire and the wheel and even a pet dinosaur. And before they knew it, they had become history's first consumers. They forgot all about life's simple pleasures like picking berries and lying in the sun, and instead put all their energy into keeping up with the Flintstones.

One day, many years later, the snake slithered by as Adam was mowing the lawn. Adam looked old and bent. No longer carefree, he was totally obsessed with duty. In fact, his whole life had become duty. "Hello there, Adam," said the snake. "How are you feeling today?"

Adam made a face. "Eck!" he said.

"And how's your meditation coming?"

Adam again made a face. "Static."

And so the separation was complete.

As Harry Cohen Baba finished his story, I began to see what my problem was. I was feeling static in my life because I was also feeling "eck!"

"Oh, Garment Centered One," I cried, "how can I heal this separation and restore the ecstatic state?"

"Since the natural order of things is ecstatic," he replied, "every time you say 'eck!' it is inevitable—static must follow. But there is a way to heal the separation. Whenever you feel that something displeases you and you are about to make that unpleasant face and say 'eck!' just exclaim, 'Eck-static!' instead. And you will always find delight in any situation."

So I tried it—and it worked! "I see delight, I see delight!" I exclaimed ecstatically. And for the first time in my life, I felt utterly at Om.

LESSON ONE: ARE YOU SUFFERING FROM TRUTH DECAY?

Scientific studies show that when people think too much—particularly when they think heavy thoughts—thought particles tend to get caught between the ears. This leads to a condition called "truth decay." Symptoms of truth decay include feelings of leadheadedness, worry, guilt, fear, negativity, and a preoccupation with time. Truth decay can begin in one small area of your life and, if unchecked, can spread from one domain to the next—until you have a full-blown case of "domain poisoning."

Are you suffering from truth decay? Take this simple quiz:

1. Are you worried that California will fall into the ocean, or worse yet, that it will be pushed?

2. When you were a child in Sunday School and saw pictures of Christians being thrown to the lions, did you feel bad because the lions in back weren't going to get any?

3. Whenever you're approached in a public place by a photographer, are you afraid he's going to want you for a "before" picture?

4. Do you figure that God probably loves you—but He's just not ready to make a commitment?

5. When you read that Universal Intelligence resides within you and can be used to solve all of your problems, do you say, "Wait a minute. Is this the same Universal Intelligence that created pro wrestling?"

6. Do you often resort to nail-biting (rather than removing them with the claw end of a hammer)?

7. As a child, were you ever afraid that you'd come home from school one day to find that your parents traded you to Pittsburgh for next year's first round draft choice?

8. Do you find you worry less than you used to, and you feel guilty about it?

9. Has your spiritual teacher told you that we are all in the process of becoming One Person—and you're afraid that person might be Howard Cosell?

10. Do you spend hours each day wishing you had more time?

0–2 "Yes" answers: You have indeed transcended many of the pitfalls of the earthly level of existence and you have already earned many frequent flyer bonus points on the higher planes.

3–5 "Yes" answers: You are definitely on the right path, but you need to enlighten up a bit.

6–8 "Yes" answers: A couple of good sessions at a soft cloth karma wash will do wonders for you.

9 or more "Yes" answers: You're a great fault-finder. Have you ever considered becoming a geologist?

The Truth About Truth Decay—Yes, There is a Cure!

It is sad indeed to watch so many people develop cavities in truth after truth until they haven't a truth left in their heads— especially when caring for your truth is so simple. Want to prevent truth decay? Then use mental floss every day. Mental floss is invisible, but you *can* feel it. Draw one end of the floss into your right ear, and listen it through to the middle of your brain until it comes out the other side. If you listen as well as most people, you should have no problem having something go in one ear and out the other. Now then, gently move the floss back and forth, and as you do so you will feel hardened ideas and putrefying thoughts dislodge. Do this twice a day and you will feel a remarkable clarity. Before long, you will be in constant touch with "Divine Truth": God is Divine, and we are the fruit of Divine, destined for grapeness.

LESSON TWO: ACHIEVING YOUR IDEAL WAIT.

Do you realize that four out of every five Americans have a serious wait problem? That's right. Studies show that most Americans can't stand waiting. (They can't even *sit* waiting.) Wait problems are being blamed for everything from heart disease to digestive disorders, high blood pressure to low income. Think about it: for every minute we spend waiting, most of us lose, on average, a minute off our lives! Ask yourself this question: Am I truly alive while I'm waiting? If the answer is no, then you've shortened your life by that much. Actually, it's not the wait itself that's harmful, but your attitude about your wait. Whenever people say to me, "I hate to wait!" I tell them they have things backward. They should wait to hate instead. And to those people who are always late because they are afraid that if they get there earlier they'll have to sit around doing nothing, I say, "Stop throwing your wait around!"

Do you have a wait problem? I have devised this simple test to help you find out. And if you can't wait to take the test, give yourself a couple of points right there.

1. Do you get upset when you buy an "instant dinner" and then find it actually takes three minutes to heat in your microwave?

2. Do you take your watch to bed with you when you make love? (Add two points if your watch is a stopwatch.)

3. Do you think it's ridiculous to wait a full nine months for a baby, and have decided to investigate Evelyn Woods' Speed Breeding course?

4. On a first date, is your opening line, "So, what graduate school would you like our grandchildren to go to?"

5. Have you given up your obsession about World War III and the Second Coming, and now find yourself thinking about World War IV and the Third Coming?

6. When a friend suggested you read *The One Minute Manager*, did you call the local college bookstore to see if they had it in Cliff Notes?

7. Do you sometimes forget to go to the bathroom for days because you didn't write it in your appointment book?

8. Do you ever record a program on your VCR and then watch the entire thing on fast forward?

9. Are you puzzled as to why no airline has instituted a Concorde flight between Cleveland and Toledo?

10. When telling jokes, do you blurt out the punchline right away because you can't wait to get to the end (premature ejoke-ulation)?

0–2 "Yes" answers: You have achieved a state of blissful waitlessness.

3–5 "Yes" answers: You are still a little burdened by your wait.

6–8 "Yes" answers: Have you tried "wait-watchers"?

9 or more "Yes" answers: You're definitely a candidate for Swami Beyondananda's Wait Training.

Swami Beyondananda's Wait Training Program

Yes, we are a society obsessed with speed. We live life by the clock. The second hand was invented about 300 years ago, and most of us have led a second-hand existence ever since. We are so concerned with what time it is, we forget that it is always now. Fortunately, I have developed a spiritual technique that allows me to transcend time and achieve a state of waitlessness. You know the theory that the key to immortality is fasting? I say the key to immortality is *slowing*. Slowing is a great metaphysical exercise because it allows you to stretch your moments—and ultimately shrink your wait.

Here's how it works. You start your slow in the morning by opening your eyes very, very slowly. You know how long it takes the sun to come up over the horizon? That's how long it should take to open your eyes. Then, cell by cell, move yourself out of bed. This should take about an hour and a half. Then ever so slowly walk into the kitchen for breakfast. How slowly? Imagine you are following in an ant's footsteps, and make sure you don't miss any. When you eat, take little gerbil bites and chew every bite until you can't remember if you took a bite or not. That's the only meal you'll have time for. If you listen to music, be sure you play all your 45s at 33⅓. Studies show that the Righteous Brothers are twenty times more relaxing to listen to than the Chipmunks. I can't guarantee that slowing will make you immortal, but I will say this—every day you do it will feel like forever.

And here are some other ways Swami's Wait Training will help you experience your perfect wait:

Breathing. Breathing can prolong your life. In fact, you will stay alive as long as you keep breathing. As Swami says in his book *Slowing Can Save Your Life,* "The process of respiration is very simple. When you breathe, you inspire. When you don't, you expire."

Metaphysical call waiting. We've all had this experience. We are waiting for a Very Important Call, and we are literally staring at the phone, waiting for it to ring. Although this sometimes can be an uncomfortable situation, actually it is an opportunity for tremendous spiritual growth. Here's how it works:

Week One: Sit by the phone and stare at it, never averting your gaze. Do not eat, do not drink, do not sleep. (You're allowed one bathroom break a day, but if you follow the other instructions, you probably won't need it.)

Week Two: Do the same thing, only this time plug the phone in.

Defiling yourself. Another thing to do while you are wait- ing is defile yourself. Yes, we have a tremendous capacity to store information. You've seen the catacombs at the library? Imagine hundreds of those, and that's what our mental filing system looks like. Not only do we use only a mere fraction of our brain cells, but we also keep many of these cells busy storing trivial information or memories that are no longer useful. That's why it's important to defile yourself and defile yourself regularly! Go through some of those files, and for goodness sake throw them out. Donate them to the brain- less! Anything! For example, are you still holding on to TV trivia from the early '60s? Are Advanced Algebra formulas that you will never use occupying valuable cranial real es- tate? And so what if you can recite in chronological order all the presidents of the United States—never mind who's who, you need every brain cell you can muster to figure out what's what.

And you can also forget every negative thing that was ever said to you, not to mention anything negative *you* might have said. Now go to the photocopy machine in the base- ment of your mind (the one on the second floor is still not working) and run off copies of every fun, inspiring, happy experience you can remember. Good. Now stick a copy in each of the mental file folders you just cleaned. Just think. In the course of waiting for a bus, you can clear out and replace dozens of stale, spoiled or downright rotten memories. And if you do your waiting where there isn't even a bus running, you can accomplish much more.

Here's what some of our graduates have been patiently waiting to tell you:

> "I used to think my perfect wait was about three minutes. Any more than that and I'd become agitated, irritable, and no fun at all. Thanks to Swami's training, I can't wait to wait."
> Nora Gretz,
> Louisville, Kentucky

> "Listen, when they gave out patience, I didn't get any because I got tired of waiting in line and left. I mean, if a person didn't pick up the phone on the second ring, I'd hang up. Until recently, whenever I'd see a red light up ahead, I'd park the car, get out, and walk. Well let me tell you, I sat through the Swami's training and now I can sit through *anything*!
> Ida Zervit,
> Fort Lee, New Jersey

> "I enjoyed your training immensely, Swami, and I now find it easy to wait anywhere. Right now, for example, I'm waiting on tables."
> Hyman Ploid,
> Denver, Colorado

So don't wait any longer! Get on our waiting list now. And hurry up—we're waiting for you!

LESSON THREE: NOTHING IS IMPORTANT

Many young seekers approach me and, seeing how peaceful I look, they say, "Boy, that enlightenment must really be something!" And I tell them, "oh, it's nothing really," and they go away marveling about how humble I am—and they miss the point. Because enlightenment is indeed Nothing. In this world of illusion, where we're fed a steady diet of Something from our first waking breath until the moment the lights go out, an empty moment just brimming over with good, clean, nonpolluting, nonstimulating Nothing can be exactly what the doctor ordered to put us in touch with the true source.

Yes, in the hustle and bustle of day-to-day existence, we often forget that Nothing is really important. How many of us spend all of our lives looking for security, when truly Nothing will make us feel secure? I bet you never realized the truth could be so simple, but here it is: Whatever your situation, relax. *Nothing will help!*

NOTHING REALLY MATTERS

How many times have you heard people say, "Nothing really matters," and you nodded in agreement. Still, most of us take Nothing for granted. But think about it. Where would we be without Nothing? Nowhere! Yes, when scientists searched for the basic building block of the universe, do you know what they found? Nothing, that's what. Sure, there are neutrons and electrons, but when you get right to the core of the matter, the atom is made up of mostly empty space. And what about outer space? Nothing separates us from the most distant planets. Why if it weren't for Nothing, we'd have Venusians living next door to us—and we can't even get along with the Iranians. If you still refuse to take Nothing seriously, consider what the world would be without Nothing:

- Pitchers couldn't pitch a shutout.
- You'd never be able to find a parking spot.
- With no cavities to fill, dentists would spend all their time on the golf course. And once they were there, they'd have to keep hitting that silly ball around forever because there'd be no hole to drop it into.
- You wouldn't be able to tell a bagel from a bialy.
- You could no longer use the excuse, "I have Nothing to wear," to avoid going to parties.
- The Know-Nothings would know something.

THE HISTORY OF NOTHING

The history of Nothing goes back a long way, at least as far back as the year "0," although there are those who believe that Nothing existed before then. No one really knows how Nothing was discovered, but it is believed that it happened when some ancient hunter inspected his traps one morning and found Nothing there. From that time on, theologians, philosophers, and of course regular old common people have had Nothing on their minds. Plato, Aristotle, and St. Thomas Aquinas all had trouble grasping it, and modern day Western philosophers from Sartre to Heidegger to Bertrand Russell have continued to grapple with Nothing. (They must have looked pretty silly but then that was before the advent of isometric exercising.) Zen Buddhist masters have based an entire philosophy on Nothing. So if you're one of those people who know Nothing about Zen, great! You're on the right track.

The Nothing Religion

Because I wholeheartedly believe that anyone who seeks the truth deserves Nothing, I have established a new religion that has Nothing at the core. It is called "Zeroastrianism," and involves the worship of the God Zeroaster, whom we believe never existed. Our motto is, "Not seeing is believing," and it is our ultimate goal to achieve Nothing. All of our efforts are for naught. Not that we make much of an effort, because an effort would be a serious violation of our One Commandment, "Thou shalt not!"

The Zeroastrian Creed

- Nothing is sacred.
- Nothing makes sense.
- Nothing lasts forever.
- Nothing works like magic.
- Nothing contains no harmful additives.
- Nothing gets out those impossible stains.
- Nothing is known to cure baldness.
- Nothing beats sex.

The Five Pathways to Oblivion

These five practices are used by serious Zeroastrians to achieve Nothing:

1. Listen to bowling on the radio.
2. Go snake hunting in Hawaii, or for that matter Ireland.
3. Visit the Embassy of Atlantis in Washington, D.C.

4. If you're an aspiring writer, get yourself a blank book. Wait for a time when you have Nothing on your mind, then write it down.

5. Get a government job.

THE NOTHING BOX: THE PORTABLE ZEROASTRIAN SHRINE

A lot of newcomers to Zeroastrianism believe that Nothing is easy, but Nothing could be further from the truth. Nothing is really difficult, and for some people Nothing is impossible! As an experiment, try thinking about Nothing. Aha! Caught you thinking about something. No sooner have you swatted that buzzing fly of maya than another one hatches and Nothing escapes your steel-trap mind. See, the mind is always trying to put things into a box, so it can't actually focus on Nothing—unless, of course, we first put Nothing in a box.

Which is exactly what I decided to do—put Nothing in a box and sell it. I figure I've worked for Nothing all these years. Why not have Nothing work for me for a change? If you're a store owner who's tired of people coming in and buying Nothing, I've got good news—now you can really sell it to them!

Indeed, Nothing is the ideal product. For years, entrepreneurs have been looking for something that's biodegradable and recyclable, something that won't deplete the earth's resources, pollute or contaminate, that isn't offensive to any political or ethnic group, that would make an excellent gift, cost next to Nothing to produce, and would last forever. It's true—Nothing fits the bill.

Unfortunately, sales have been slow. Even though it has been touted as an excellent gift ("Nothing's too good for your friends, but give it to them anyway"), and passes the most stringent quality-control standards ("We do Nothing right or we don't do Nothing at all"), people have been reluctant to spend their money on Nothing. And yet, so many of us continue to fill our lives with the most ridiculous kinds of "somethings"—ranging from "Garbage Pail Kids" for the little ones to gourmet pet foods (although the idea of canning gourmets has its appeal) to B-1 bombers—even though, ultimately, Nothing will buy us peace of mind.

FIVE GOOD REASONS TO BUY A BOX OF NOTHING

1. If you're the kind of person who worries about everything you have, get this for yourself—and you'll have Nothing to worry about.

2. If you stop to consider the old Russian proverb, "He who has Nothing, owes Nothing," you will see that this product is a foolproof safeguard against being in debt.

3. Unlike the rest of your possessions, you *will* be able to take it with you when you go.

4. If you are plagued by neighbors who play loud '50s music while you're trying to sleep, there's good news: Nothing can stop the Duke of Earl.

5. And if you like Nothing better than money, that's great. The Swami likes money better than Nothing!

Swami Answers All Your Unasked Questions About Nothing

Dear Swami:
After years and years of dieting, I've come to the conclu-sion that Nothing will help me lose weight. What do you think?

Lou Zwait,
Royal Gorge, Colorado

Dear Lou:

As you may already know, gaining and losing weight is purely psychological. We gain weight due to an unresolved edible complex—we think something is edible and we put it in our mouth—and if we swallow, we are done for. Then all we can think about is our waistline, and that makes us even fatter because it is a spiritual principle that what we think about expands. That is why the old saying is true: The waist is a terrible thing to mind.

Yes, when it comes to dieting, absolutely Nothing works. That is why I recommend the Nothing Diet. Unlike most diets, where you learn to eat only until you are full, the Nothing Diet teaches you to eat only until you are empty. Nothingburgers are the official Nothing Diet food. With Nothingburgers there's no need to wonder where the beef is, because our motto is, "You got no beef with us." And for really holesome eating, try doughnut holes for dessert. Sure, you were taught to eat around them as a kid, but really, the holes are the best part (particularly when you consider what ingredients go into the average doughnut).

★

Dear Swami:

I've tried everything, but Nothing satisfies my husband. What should I do?

Amanda B. Reckondwith,
Newport News, Virginia

Dear Amanda:

You're lucky that he is so easily satisfied. I suggest that you give him all the Nothing he can handle.

★

Dear Swami:

I've been told I should try to do Nothing, but no matter what I do, I always seem to be doing something. What do you suggest?

Frieda Knight,
Detroit, Michigan

Dear Frieda:

First, make a "Not To Do" list. Then don't do the items on the list. Then throw away the list. Repeat as often as necessary, and you'll be accomplishing Nothing in no time.

★

Dear Swami:

Nothing was bothering me, so I went to the doctor and now I find I'm allergic to Nothing. What should I do?
                                        Noah Parent Reason,
                                        San Diego, California

Dear Noah:

That's Nothing to sneeze at. It isn't easy to avoid a void. If I were you, I'd stay away from wide open spaces and eat a lot of solid food.

★

Dear Swami:

Is it true that nature abhors a vacuum?
                                        Penny R. Cade,
                                        Charlotte, North Carolina

Dear Penny:

I know that's what all the gossip columnists say, but I think it's an exaggeration. Let's just say you shouldn't invite them to the same party.

★

LESSON FOUR: SWAMI'S OM IMPROVEMENT TECHNIQUES

It's too bad so many people are living in the past tense, the present tense, and the future tense because there's really no need to be tense at all. Fortunately, many hard-driving achievers have realized the importance of relaxation, so they've gritted their teeth in fierce determination and declared, "I'm going to be the most relaxed damned person I know!" Groups have formed in the workplace to help people relax, and some even have contests to see who can get more relaxed. And sales of the U.S. Marine Corps Relaxation Program tape are booming ("RELAX YOUR FEET!" "YES-SUH!" "I CAN'T *HEAR* YOU . . ." "FEET ARE RELAXED, SUH!"). Yes, learning to relax can be stressful—but it doesn't have to be. That is why I have devised these specific Om Improvement techniques and products to help you achieve your perfect wait, overcome truth decay, and make sure Nothing works for you:

The Marcel Marceau "Sound of Silence" meditation album. You ain't heard Nothing until you've heard this album. Aficionados of the NoTown sound will particularly appreciate Marceau's rendition of the title tune, along with "Nothing's Too Good For My Baby," "Quiet Village," "Nothing But Heartaches," "Nowhere Man," "Silence Is Golden," "No Reply," "I Who Have Nothing," "It's Not For Me To Say," and of course that all-time classic, "I Got Plenty of Nothin'." His rendition of "Nothing From Nothing Leaves Nothing," is a real hand-clapper (one hand, please). Lip-sync version available on VCR.

Nothing software. Add years to the life of your computer by teaching it to meditate. Available for all computers. Warning: Please limit use to no more than forty minutes per day. Manufacturers are not responsible if computer disappears, transmutes, or turns into a Hare Krishna.

Numbskull. Developed by the reknowned physician Dr. Hugh Manitarian (his "Sex and Canteloupe Diet" book was a sensation several years ago), Numbskull is a long-lasting anesthetic that will allow you to experience Nothing for months. Imagine how refreshed you'll feel after Numbskull erases all your tapes and cleans your head! You'll feel a lot less "eck"—and a lot less static.

The official nothing vacation at Camp Omward Bound. If you're one of those people with no time to relax and no money to spend, you can save time and money by taking the official Nothing vacation at Camp Omward Bound. If your whole life has been outward bound or up-ward bound, maybe it's time you went Om. Located on a flat, boring lot near Om Aha, Nebraska, Camp Omward Bound helps you feel free to explore your inner self, because *it* is free—free of mountains, lakes, trees, and any external stimulation. Concerned about social life at Camp Omward Bound? Don't be, because there isn't any. At Camp Omward Bound, our motto is, "One's company, two's a crowd."

And you'll love our "Nothing ventured, Nothing gained" fitness program featuring such Nothing Olympic events as the 220-yard Dead Man's Float, the One Night Stand (which involves standing for one night without moving), the Bench Press (that's where you sit and press your gluteus maximum against the bench), and of course, the Decafalon (where you drink decaffeinated coffee and try to stay awake through Andy Warhol movies). At Camp Omward Bound, we *live* the official Nothing Olympics motto: "No Sweat!"

A vacation at Camp Omward Bound is guaranteed to leave you eager to return to work, and just as refreshed as if you had no vacation at all! For half-price, you can take your vacation at home and leave Nothing to the imagination.

Swami Answers All Your Questions on Om Improvement Techniques

Dear Swami:

Okay, so we've had the Harmonic Convergence and the World Instant of Cooperation. Astrologers say we've officially entered the Age of Aquarius. My question is, when are things really going to change? I'm getting impatient already.

Anna Cheever,
Evanston, Illinois

Dear Anna:

Actually, in recent years there have been two powerful signs that mainstream society is waking up to the New Age. First, Shirley MacLaine was asked to leave her aura print at Graumann's Chinese Theater. The second incident occurred during the 1988 World Series. Vin Scully and Joe Garagiola were announcing. Vin Scully said, "Kirk Gibson was a strike-out victim his last time at bat." And Garagiola replied, "No, Vin, there *are* no victims. Kirk actually created that strikeout for his own spiritual advancement."

★

Dear Swami:

I'm in a program here at the University where I'm learning to be an orchestra conductor. The problem is, I have a hard time taking criticism. My professors all tell me I'm being resistant, and I keep saying, "No way!" Now I'm in danger of flunking and what I want to know is, do you think my resistance has anything to do with it?

Gail Force-Wind,
Ann Arbor, Michigan

Dear Gail:

I have always been an advocate of the path of least resistance, and this is no exception. No wonder you are flunking!

Obviously, your tremendous resistance makes you a very poor conductor. Since this is a highly charged issue with you, I suggest that each time you feel a surge of resistance, you chant the mantra, "Ohm."

★

Dear Swami:

I understand you've uncovered the secret of physical immortality. Is there any truth to this rumor? Do you think physical immortality is appropriate? And can you share any suggestions you might have for increasing one's life span?

Lon Gevity,
Pensacola, Florida

Dear Lon:

It is true. I have indeed discovered one of the secrets of physical immortality. It all started with a near-death experience I had a number of years ago. I was working at a cemetery, so I was near Death a lot, and one day Death came over to introduce itself. I must have appeared a little frightened, because Death reassured me that it was not my time, as I still had many things to do on this plane of existence. It was then that I hit on the secret of immortality—procrastination. So I made myself a "Things To Do" list that you would not believe, and each day I don't do most of the items on the list (except for those I *really* enjoy). That way, if Death calls I can say, "You know, I'm just swamped this month. But stay in touch. Maybe we'll do lunch sometime."

Actually, I have good news for everyone reading this who is currently inhabiting a body (channeled entities excluded). You are *already* physically immortal! The way I figure it, mortality and immortality are polar opposites—if you have one, you cannot have the other. Since the only way to prove you are mortal is by dying, then clearly you are immortal—so far. Of course, at any time you may choose to join the Mortal Majority and step off the planet anyway, and that is an acceptable choice too. Shortly before he made his transition

(*Note:* When asked how they would like to die, four out of five new agers said they prefer "making their transition" to "croaking") I asked my guru Harry Cohen Baba how he felt about physical immortality. He shrugged and said, "Listen, I have a higher plane I want to catch. Besides, everybody needs samadhi sometime."

★

Dear Swami:
I'd like to believe all these new age ideas, but it's difficult when I see the negativity around me everywhere. On the global scale, there's war, starvation, hatred between nations. On the national level, there's scandal, corruption, drug abuse, homeless people—I could go on and on. And even in our everyday dealings with people, there's mistrust, jealousy, criticism. Swami, what's the purpose of all this negative stuff?
                                        Curran T. Ventz,
                                        Bethesda, Maryland

Dear Curran:
    Life is like photography. You use the negative to develop. You know how when you're developing pictures, you dip the negative into a solution, and you get a positive image? Well, in life there's a solution that will help you turn the negative into a positive—and the solution is love. With love you can turn all your negatives into the handsome prints you've been waiting for.

★

Dear Swami:
With all the hustle and bustle in life, I find it really hard to just be quiet and centered within. What do you suggest for finding that quieter place?
                                        Ann Feddiman,
                                        Long Beach, California

Dear Ann:

You obviously need to do some Omwork. First, stand quietly for a few moments. Then click your heels three times and repeat, "There's no place like Om, there's no place like Om, there's no place like Om." You will instantly be transported to a quieter place—Kansas.

☆

PART TWO

Looking Out
for Number Two:
Swami's Guide
to Being on the Path

Now THAT YOU HAVE CLEARED YOUR MIND, you are ready to embark upon the path and taste of the tree of knowledge— but first you must learn to discriminate so that you are not embarking up the wrong tree. Yes, there is a seeker born every minute and two to take him along the path. And it is not easy being on the path, because the path is strewn with obstacles. You must watch very carefully where you step, which is why I include this chapter called, "Looking Out For Number Two." You know how people on the path are always talking about releasing this and letting go of that? Well, that is why *this* Swami does not go barefoot. This chapter will help you avoid stepping into three of the messiest pitfalls along the path: Oughtism, Growth Out, and Emotion Sickness.

Lesson Five: Beware of Oughtism

A lot of people say the problem with the world today is the "Me" Generation, where everyone is out doing what they want to do. I say the real problem is the "Who Me?" Generation, which is people out doing what *everyone else* wants them to do. And this condition, which I call Oughtism, is the most rampant epidemic on the planet today. Oughtism is a disease of the oughtanomic nervous system where the unfortunate victims oughtamatically do what others tell them they ought to do. If left untreated, Oughtism can result in a total loss of the ability to think. Fortunately, there is an organization called S.T.O.P.—Society to Transcend Oughtistic Practices—which has made it their mission to end Oughtism on the planet by the year 2000. I'll tell you how pervasive this epidemic is. When people find out about the crusade to end Oughtism, the first thing they ask, "What do you think I ought to do about it?"

How Swami Cured Himself of Oughtism

When I was young, I didn't know what I wanted to be. Oh, I had the usual childhood aspirations—I wanted to be a nurse or an Indian princess or a housewife. That was before I found out I was a boy. When I found that out, I decided I wanted to be a cowboy. All my friends wanted to be cowboys, and my parents thought I should become a cowboy. So one summer I took a job as a cowpuncher. Now to be perfectly accurate, I never had to actually punch a cow, although a few times I did have to jab one with my finger. So technically, I was just a cowpoke. But I didn't like it very much. Cows are boring. They're pretty much into their own thing. And if you aren't careful where you step, you are, too.

Being an idealist in those days, I went to my high school counselor and told her I was looking for a career where I could fight the decay I saw around me, where I could make an impression on people, fill the empty spaces in their lives, and build bridges. "I've got the perfect career for you," she said. "Become a dentist." The next summer I took a job assisting a dentist. My job was to prepare the novocaine needles. One day, as an experiment, I decided to leave the novocaine out to see if the placebo effect worked. It didn't. You could hear the screams across the state of Oklahoma. I left dentistry that day, but I had learned a valuable spiritual technique: Transcend Dental Medication.

Over the next several years, I went from counselor to counselor trying to find out what I was supposed to do. "Get into communications," one said. So I got a job working for the phone company, telling the time. I got fired from that job one day when they caught me not watching the clock. "You should get a government job," said another counselor, so I got a job as a census taker. I quit that job because I hated those embarrassing personal questions you had to ask people—like, "List all members of your family broken down by sex."

On the advice of a friend, I got a job as a vacuum cleaner salesman, but it was around that time I met my guru, Harry Cohen Baba, and he told me to give up all my attachments—so I had to quit that job as well. There I was, my children: no job, no direction, not even enough money to call the phone company to tell them I couldn't pay my bill. I threw myself at my guru's feet (I was a pretty good tackle in high school) and said, "Oh, Garment Centered One, tell me what I should do!"

"Listen here, boychick," he replied, getting up and dusting himself off, "you are letting everyone else make your decisions for you. Don't just follow someone else's oughtas. What you should do is stand on your own two feet and think for yourself."

So I did exactly as he said. I stood on that streetcorner for days, thinking. I won't go into all the trouble I had with the dogs and pigeons, but some garment workers mistook me for a mannequin and I came home with a lovely suit. Anyway, after many days of not eating, I felt a mysterious, unearthly presence close by. There, in front of me, I saw the vision of one of my earliest spiritual teachers, Andy Devine. Yes, it is true. I had spent my formative years chanting his mantra, "Yer durn tootin'," and whenever I had a problem, I would meditate on his picture on my cereal box, hoping for some Devine Guidance.

"Say there, young feller," he rasped, "looks like yer in a heap o' trouble. How can I help yuh?"

"Oh, Devine One," I answered, "my guru instructed me to stand on my own two feet and think for myself, and I've been standing here and thinking for the past week and a half. I actually think he's forgotten about me, and I don't know what to do next. I know you can help me!"

"Wal' son, sorta reminds me of a movie I was in many years back called *Shoot Out at the I'm-Okay-You're-Okay Corral.* It was about two o' these gu-ru fellers fightin' over which one would be the only Universal Law west of the Pecos. They were a-fussin' and a-feudin' for days, with groups of cowboys camped in front of each of their hash-rams shoutin' the praises of their particular gu-ru. Now yuh see, I played the part of the cook and I was welcome in both camps, 'cuz I was the only one who could make biscuits and gravy macrobiotic-style. Wal' anyhow, one day their carryin' on got me so gol-durn flustered that I burned the dang gomazio. That did it! I got up on the hill between camps and I sez, 'Now lissen up, you fellers, you're a-fightin' over somethin' downright foolish. Ain't no gu-ru knows anymore than you do. Shucks, even the word gu-ru can tell yuh that. Just spell it out: G-U-R-U. Gee, you are you! Now stop all yer fussin' and I'll fix you all a heapin' pot o' miso stew!' "

And in a flash, my Devine vision was gone, and the realization hit me—there was no need to wait for others to tell me what to do, I was my own guru! All the answers I sought were within *me*! (Although it would be several years before I figured out what the corresponding questions were.) Flushed with joy and insight, I rushed into the ashram and told Harry Cohen Baba what had happened. "Is it true, oh Garment Centered One?" I asked. "Am I truly my own guru?"

"What do you think I've been trying to tell you all these months?" he asked. "Listen, I'll tell you a story which has been passed down among Men of the Cloth since the first stitch of clothing was worn. In the beginning, we say, was the Naked Truth. And God saw that this was good, but also realized that the Universe He created was an expanding Universe. And if the Universe was going to be going out all the time, It would need nice clothes. So God created clothing, and boy did He have fun playing dress-up with the World. Especially hats. God had a great time making hats. And when He finally rested on the Seventh Day, He saw how nice the World looked all dressed up and exclaimed, 'Now this World is ready to go someplace!'

"And what a variety of garments there were! In those days nobody knew from color-coordinated. Did you know that the first socks didn't have to match? Anyway, after many thousands of years there came the Dark Ages. In the Dark Ages, pastels were out, blacks, browns, and greys were in. Dark clothing became like a uniform, and uniformity became a habit. As a matter of fact, that's when nuns started wearing habits, and some of these habits persist to this day.

"But in this New Age we are entering, it is time for us to shed our old habits. Don't wait to be fitted into some uniform. Suit yourself!"

"You mean," I asked, "There's no longer a need to tailor our beliefs after someone else's fashion? That we must decide what fits for us?"

"Yer darn tootin'!" said the Garment Center Saint.

ARE YOU OUGHTISTIC? TAKE THIS SIMPLE TEST

1. Do you feel you should get married even though you don't want to get married and there isn't even anyone to get married to?
2. Do you feel obligated to give blood even when you're down to your last pint?
3. Do you put on clean underwear every day just in case you get hit by a car and have to go to the hospital?
4. Have you ever accidentally ripped the tag off of a mattress or pillow and gone to the local station house and turned yourself in?
5. Do you find yourself taking thirds of things you don't like at all-you-can-eat buffets because you don't want the cooks to feel bad?
6. Have you taken an extra job to help pay off the national debt?
7. Did you recently buy a condo in Colorado that you're never going to use, just so you could get a free toaster?
8. If you're leaving for vacation for a few weeks, do you always make sure a friend comes in to feed the roaches?

9. Do you still raise your hand before going to the bathroom?

10. Are you reading this only because someone said you ought to?

0–2 "Yes" answers: You are an independent thinker who realizes that what other people think about you is none of your business.

3–5 "Yes" answers: You still pay too much attention to the opinions of others. If you're afraid of what people will think, there's good news—most people don't think!

6–7 "Yes" answers: You can't expect to fly the higher planes if you are on oughtamatic pilot most of the time. You oughta take the controls for a change.

8 or more "Yes" answers: You are truly an oughtomaton. You are one of those people who will try to justify your life by saying, "But I was only following oughtas."

Swami's Plan for Combating Oughtism

If you answered any of the above questions "yes," you could be Oughtistic. But you really shouldn't feel bad because you're not alone. An estimated 40 million Americans suffer from this silent crippler. And most of them don't even notice. Fortunately, Oughtism *can* be cured. But first, you must recognize its five warning signals:

• Any involuntary nodding of the head up and down, especially when someone asks for volunteers.

• Sharp pangs of guilt after ingesting a chocolate chip cookie.

• Any enlargement of the onus.

• An empty feeling between the ears.

• Constriction of the intestines—that duty-bound feeling.

So join us, won't you? Let's stop this epidemic of Oughtism before our whole society comes under the spell of oughto-suggestion. When the person with the S.T.O.P. sign comes to your door, give and give generously. You really ought to.

SWAMI BEYONDANANDA'S NO AWARENESS TRAINING

Are you hiding your true feelings from others?

Do you say YES when you mean MAYBE and MAYBE when you mean NO?

Have you been suffering from Oughtism for years, and your friends tell you you really should do something about it?

If you've tried every way there is and nothing has worked, maybe it's time for you to try the—

NO WAY!

The No Awareness Seminar is designed to help you experience complete No-ingness. Obligations, agreements, requests bothering you? Whatever it is, Just Say No! I don't know why they have this "Just Say No" mantra hooked up with drugs. If people just said no when they meant no, they wouldn't *need* drugs!

It all started back when we were toddlers. As two-year-olds, we were just beginning to say NO and really enjoy it. Then what do you think happened? Our parents told us saying NO wasn't nice and to stop it or they'd break our heads. Now what kind of choice is that? Since that time, we've been saying YES when we've really wanted to say NO. So I say, say YES to NO, for it is written, "To seek the scent of the correct path, follow your NOs, for your NOs will set you free."

Just Say No!

Yes, there's no awareness like No Awareness. Saying NO not only feels good, but it's good for you too. Just saying that simple mantra, "NO-O-O-O-O!" can ward off many common afflictions, including telephone solicitors, chain letters disguised as new age business opportunities, door-to-door religious proselytizers, and personal growth seminars which insist that if you really knew how to think for yourself, you would sign up.

The best way to throw off the yoke of oughtamatic feelings of obligation is to practice this healing mantra daily. To be a slave to obligation is to NO nothing! As you practice, you will find you NO more and more, until one day you will finally NO it all!

To NO 'Em is to Love 'Em

Who to practice saying NO to:

Your loved ones. That's right. Saying NO to those close to you fosters unconditional love. If they can still love you after you've denied them everything, their love *must* be unconditional!

Political candidates. Last I heard, the Democrats were still trying to show they were for the "little guy," and had proposed a bill that would provide free housing to homeless people under 5'2"—Stay Free Mini-Pads, they would be called. Meanwhile, the Republicans were blaming acid rain on Timothy Leary. And those $1000-a-plate dinners you hear about? No wonder our taxes are so high. If they are spending this kind of money on dishes, imagine what they'll spend on bombers!

Panhandlers. Panhandlers are lazy and shiftless, and should not be encouraged. If they had any ambition, they'd be out stealing.

Any organization with "ANONYMOUS" **in the name.** Be wary of any group designed to help you get rid of your addiction to some substance—and replace it with an addiction to the group. These identified addictions are endless. The latest one that I heard about is for people who are addicted to feeling like nobodies. It is called "Anonymous Anonymous."

Your boss. Consistently saying No to your boss can have great spiritual consequences because it will speed up your release of attachment to material possessions.

Charitable organizations. Next time someone calls you and says they are collecting money for heart disease, say, "I am sorry, but I am against heart disease." And hang up.

Gurus. Next time you have the urge to follow a guru because you think he or she knows more than you, stop whatever you are doing, look in the mirror, and do the "Guru Chant." It goes: "G-U-R-U, G-U-R-U, G-U-R-U—Gee, you are you!" Believe me, gurus will thank you, too. I, for one, have no followers, because frankly I get paranoid when I think I am being followed. When people cluster around me, I get nervous (a mild case of clusterphobia which I developed in New York). And when people swoon and say, "Oh Swami, I want to bathe in your darshan," I say, "Never mind. Last time you bathed in my darshan you left a ring around it!"

And Above All, NO Thyself!

To become spiritually disciplined and a true No Aware Man (or Woman), you must learn to say No. Whatever your desires, deny yourself! Of course, if you're a masochist who lusts after self-denial, you must deny yourself the pleasure of denying yourself. For you, a strict regimen of strong drink, late-night parties and rich desserts is in order.

Now You Too Can Truly be No-Aware!

Here's what the No Awareness Seminar will do for you:

- Help you relive your toilet training. (*Note:* Please bring rubber pants and an extra set of diapers.)
- Help you lose weight.
- Help you get rid of unwanted friends, lovers, possessions, and employment.
- Teach you to say NO before you're even asked.

And here's what they are saying about the No Awareness Training:

> "No."
> "No, thanks."
> "No way, buster!"
> "NO!"
> "Absolutely not!"
> "Forget it!"
> "Are you kidding?"

And from one of our drop outs:

> "Well, maybe. . . ."

Say NO to the No Awareness Seminar (but take it anyway). And if you've already agreed to take it, great—you *really* need it!

Of course, sometimes it isn't enough to NO everything. Some Oughtistic patterns are more ingrained than others. And there are simply some people who won't take NO for an answer. Then what? If you're looking for more drastic measures to deal with Oughtism, look no further than

SWAMI BEYONDANANDA'S "RUDE AWAKENING" TRAINING

Free yourself forever from the yoke of politeness! Let your natural desire to be rude express itself!

Yes, for years we've learned to be polite, regardless of what we're really feeling. Rudeness is a natural impulse and each time we repress it, we cause ourselves permanent damage. That's right. People who are overly polite are more likely to get sick and they are also more likely to be bothered by pests who can't take a subtle hint.

Drawing on the teachings and techniques of such rude awakened masters as Don Rickles, Rasputin, Groucho Marx, George Steinbrenner, and Attila the Hun, our rudeness experts will show you:

- How to be late.
- How to break agreements and blame the other person.
- Loudness and interrupting—two surefire ways of being heard.
- Spilling hot coffee—the way to make your colleagues stand up and take notice.
- How rudeness can increase your driving pleasure.
- Pushing ahead in line—the best way to get there first.

What they are saying about the Rude Awakening Training (R.A.T.):

"Rudeness helped me work through my fear of being alone. Since I've learned rudeness, I'm alone all the time."
                                        —H.C., Unpleasantville, N.Y.

"I never forget a face, but in your case I'll make an exception."
                                        —G.M., Hollywoodlawn, Cal.

"I've always been outwardly very polite, while I seethed with the inner desire to be rude and obnoxious. Thank you for letting the real me out of the closet!"
                                        —J.M., Flushing, N.Y.

And from one of our most successful graduates:

"Your training is a total rip-off, and Swami Beyondananda is an egotistical charlatan!"
                                        —W.E., Caramel Center, Cal.

Special bonus! Sign up for the Rude Awakening Training right now, and we'll send you, at no extra charge, our videotape on "Punk Yoga"—that's where you stand on *somebody else's* head. And as an added bonus, we promise to call you for the next five Sunday mornings—at 6:00 A.M.—and play selected excerpts from the critically acclaimed *Twisted Sister Does Sinatra* album so that you can truly experience Rude Awakening.

LESSON SIX: DEALING WITH GROWTH-OUT

There is another serious condition that often afflicts those on the path who have had too much personal growth. It is called "Growth-Out." Yes, there are some really "growthed out" people in the human potential movement, and it's a serious problem. Now I have nothing against the human potential movement—I think we really do have the potential to be human. But, my goodness, there are so many paths to choose from, you can get spiritual indigestion from swallowing too many different beliefs. Are you biting off more than you can choose? Take the following quiz:

1. Did you recently sign up and pay for a seminar on How To Improve Your Memory—and then forget to go?

2. Have you spent so much money on fixing yourself that now you're *really* broke?

3. Do you spend so much time out of your body that you're thinking of renting it out to a disembodied entity?

4. Have you expanded your mind so much that you had to call in a shrink just so you can fit through your door?

5. Did you enthusiastically declare to your partner at a growth seminar, "I totally support you!" and now that person expects you to pay his/her rent?

6. Did you sign up for a class on "Drawing on the Right Side of Your Brain," then quickly dropped it when you heard you'd have to shave half your head for a smoother drawing surface?

7. Did you get rolfed because you heard it would lead to detachment, and now you find it detached your muscle from your ligaments, your cartilage from your bone?

8. Did you pay $500 for a firewalking seminar only to find at the last minute you had coaled feet?

9. Do you go from yoga teacher to yoga teacher, constantly seeking greener postures?

10. Do you think you might be confused—but you're just not sure?

0–2 "Yes" answers: You are predictable, reliable, practical, and down-to-earth. In other words, you've probably never taken a personal growth seminar in your life. To you, "new age" is something you are on your next birthday.

3–5 "Yes" answers: You are showing the first signs of Growth Out; you're getting a little frayed at the edges. So, just sit back, relax—and don't be 'frayed.

6–8 "Yes" answers: You are experiencing a great deal of confusion in your life. If you're not careful where you park your karma, it might well get towed away.

Over 8 "Yes" answers: You are growthly disturbed.

UNDERSTANDING GROWTH-OUT: THE PRINCIPLES OF CONFUSIONISM

Growth is like a road map. Unfolding is no problem. It's getting it all folded up again that is so frustrating. One of the surefire symptoms of Growth Out is confusion. Confusion can be confusing, but it is a natural stage while on the path. As my own beloved guru, Harry Cohen Baba, used to say, "On the subway to enlightenment, confusion is the next-to-last stop. So if you're confused, stay on for one more station."

In fact, there is an entire belief system founded on the power of confusion, called Confusionism. Based on the teachings of the great Eastern master, Confuse-us, Confusionism maintains that chaos is a good thing. (Or maybe it isn't. He wasn't really clear on that.) Said Confuse-us in one of his more lucid moments, "Entropy—or deterioration—is the natural state of the physical world. So why not go directly to chaos, sit down, have a smoke, and wait patiently for the rest of the world to get there?"

Little is known about the early years of Confuse-us, although in his autobiography, *Don't Believe A Word I Say,* he tells us he spent the first eight years of his life thinking he was the family dog. His mother described him as an unusual child with "a fetching personality."

During his twenties, Confuse-us decided to be a wandering minstrel. But he had such severe anxiety attacks before going on the road that he never actually performed. Unfortunately, no one could help him with his affliction, since at the time there was no cure for pre-minstrel syndrome. His thirties were spent immersed in worldly debauchery, drinking heavily as he hobnobbed with the Roman hot tub set. So great was his lust for drink, that some nights he would drain an entire hot tub.

Confuse-us began to suffer bouts of omnesia—that is where you remember everything—and he furiously began writing it all down. The result was his most monumental book, *Everything You Always Wanted To Know.* Says Harry Cohen Baba, who himself puzzled over Confusionism in his early years, "It was a truly amazing book. Five thousand pages, and not a sentence made sense. But in a very definite way, it helped raise humankind to new levels and provided us with much spiritual food. I know this from personal experience because my own little boy used to stand on this book to reach the cookie jar."

It was during the next period of Confuse-us's life that he traveled the globe encouraging followers to utter his simple mantra: "Huh?" He also gave the world his best known book, *The Power of Incompletion,* which, alas, was never finished. Tragically, Confuse-us was practicing out-of-body travel one day and he simply forgot where he parked his body. By the time he got back there, his battery was burned out. But he leaves us with his legacy of incompletion, and with Confusionism's most profound teaching—"Just say 'what?' "

SWAMI'S CURE FOR GROWTH-OUT—THE INCOMPLETION TRAINING

So one way to combat the confusion that comes from Growth-Out is to embrace the confusion, give it a big fat kiss on the face, and relax in the knowledge that this confusion will pass—only to be replaced by newer, more advanced confusion. That is why I have developed the "Incompletion Training—the Seminar That Never Ends," to put the principles of Confusionism into practice in your life. Yes, by the time you've decided you've had enough of this seminar, you'll be so bewildered, baffled, and perplexed that you'll have no choice but to stumble into the light.

Why is incompletion so powerful? Because we are a society obsessed with *completion*. Look at how we let appointment books rule our lives. Appointment books are unnatural! Think about it. Do the swallows have an appointment book in which they write, "Return to Capistrano" under "Things To Do"? No, but they still get there on schedule. Isn't that what time management is all about? You people who think you are managing your time by looking at your watch all the time—maybe time is managing *you*. Real time management is being like the child playing hide-and-seek—you must lose yourself in the game.

It's interesting how Americans think that lists and details and completing things have something to do with enlightenment. But it's just not true. Take the great spiritual masters, the avatars. I know it's not true because I know these guys personally. I see them *every year* at the Ascended Masters Golf Tournament. For example, Jesus hardly ever finished everything on his plate. Mohammed always forgot to take out the garbage. Buddha was three years behind in his monthly karma payments. Meher Baba never completed a sentence. And you want to know the real reason why Moses went into the desert? To avoid creditors. Now, of course you never knew these things. Do you think your mother is going to tell you that Jesus didn't finish everything on his plate? I was no different from you, my children. I too was obsessed with completion—until I had an experience that changed my life.

How Swami Learned About Incompletion

When I first met Harry Cohen Baba, I was still working with the Farmer's Union—the E.I.E.I.O. But the Garment Centered One suggested that if I wanted to be a true Man of the Cloth, the textile trades might suit me better. It turned out to be a close-knit group, and I fit right in. My job was sewing pockets on shirts. I had utter faith in the Garment Center credo— "as a man sews, so shall he reap"—so I set to work to be the best pocket-stitcher in the business.

I had heard that the average pocket-stitcher was able to do 35 pockets an hour, so I made it my goal to do 50. The first few days I spent learning the workings of the sewing machine. Once I accidentally stitched my tie to a shirt making its way down the assembly line. My co-workers nicknamed me "Isadora," and from that time on I wore turtlenecks.

By the first Friday, I was working like the fury. I could see my co-workers getting a little irked with me for showing them up, but I figured that was their karma. At the end of five hours, I had stitched my day's quota of 250 shirt-pockets. Was I proud! Surely I would be commended. So I called my boss over. He nodded and said, "Mmm-hmm."

"Aren't you going to commend me?" I asked.

"Commend you?" he said, in his thick Yiddish accent. "Only God can give Commendments, and ten of those is more than we can handle. Me, I give suggestions. So I strongly suggest that *your* daily quota is now 350!"

And that is why I remember what my beloved teacher Harry Cohen Baba used to say: "Look, you start something, it's a beginning. But complete it, and you're finished!"

The Magic of Incompletion

Have you ever stopped to think how empty our lives would be if everything were complete?

- There'd be no reason to get up except to wind the clock and feed the cat.
- There'd be no leftovers.
- There'd be no more pleasant surprises, like finding a $20 bill in the pocket of a pair of pants you didn't even know you had.
- Pass defenders in football would have to find another line of work.
- And you could just forget soap operas.

If everything were already complete, Robert Frost would have no promises to keep and he could just crawl off and sleep in the snow and nobody would even notice. So I say to you, never finish anything. That's confusion, you tell me. And I tell you that if the road to hell is paved with good intentions, the road to heaven is paved with confusion.

Here are some of the things people who have begun the Incompletion Training are saying:

Dear Swami:
    Your Incompletion Training is superb. Just as you suggested, I'm looking at the turmoil, incompletion, and confusion in my life as the last stage before enlightenment. I hope enlightenment comes soon, because I forgot to pay my bill and now they're about to shut off my electricity.
                                        Bill Stupay,
                                        Eugene, Oregon

Dear Swami:
    Love your training! And the thing I love most is—hey, listen—it's been good talking to you. I'll write some other time.
                                        Lou Sends,
                                        Overland Park, Kansas

Dear Swami:
    Just a note to tell you

So take the Incompletion Seminar, and watch your limiting beliefs in orderly progress and completion unravel, not to mention your life. And when you reach the point where you feel fully incomplete . . . well, you're not quite there yet.

GROWTH-OUT TREATMENT NUMBER TWO: A SIMPLE PILL THAT ELIMINATES CONFUSION ONCE AND FOR ALL

Do you suffer from nagging doubts? Tired of being wrong all the time? Do confusion and uncertainty keep you awake nights?

Confusion is powerful, all right, but it is not for everyone. Thinking for yourself can get awfully lonely, especially at night. You want some nice warm beliefs to curl up with and what do you have instead? Icy doubts and cold confusion. As you know, the road to heaven is paved with confusion, and sometimes you need something to pick yourself up off the pavement. That's when I reach for my little bottle of Ortho-Dox. Yes, Ortho-Dox Brand Corrective Beliefs, for the temporary relief of confusion, doubt, and headaches due to excessive thinking. Ortho-Dox is guaranteed to dissolve nagging doubts, gut-level feelings, even logic—or we'll double your confusion back.

Just pop one into your mouth and you'll feel Ortho-Dox's tiny little time-released dogmas go to work instantly on even the most stubborn doubts. Its gentle, soothing action dissolves uncertainty in minutes, then puts up an invisible protective shield which makes you impervious to new ideas for a full twenty-four hours. Taken regularly, Ortho-Dox is guaranteed to close your mind permanently!

And here's a sample of what our thousands of satisfied customers are saying about Ortho-Dox:

> Dear Swami:
> I used to wake up in the morning, fold my hands and pray for rain. I had a head full of ideas that were driving me insane. So I went to see the gypsy. "How are you?" he said to me, and I said, "There's too much confusion. I can't get no relief." So he gave me a bottle of Ortho-Dox and I'm a changed man. I no longer need a weatherman to know which way the wind blows. I don't think twice . . . and it's all right.
> B.Z., Woodstock, N.Y.

So if you find confusion hard to swallow, try swallowing one of these—Ortho-Dox Brand Corrective Beliefs, now in these great flavors:

New Age	Catholic	Existentialist
Freudian	Hare Krishna	Vegetarian
Anarchist	Jewish	Buddhist
Leninist	Shiite	Methodist
Lennonist	He-ite	Rhythm-Methodist

and introducing our newest and most popular flavor. . . Good ol' Bible-Thumpin', Heathen-Stompin' Fundamentalist!

And for those really, really *deep-seated* doubts, try Ortho-Dox suppositories. That's Ortho-Dox, "the next best thing to enlightenment."

LESSON SEVEN: TREATING EMOTION SICKNESS

Even if you successfully resist having gurus oughta you around and feel totally complete feeling incomplete, the path still has its ups and downs. Sometimes the elevator ride through the highrise of consciousness can cause emotion sickness—that dizzying feeling of not being in control. Are you suffering from emotion sickness? Take this simple quiz:

1. Do you take to your bed for days and refuse visitors when your favorite soap opera character dies?
2. Have you gotten so caught up in past-life work that you've actually gone and gotten a part-time job in a previous incarnation?
3. When you attended a prosperity seminar and were told that there's an "ocean of abundance," did you wonder how you managed to get stuck in the Bermuda Triangle?

4. Did you take a class in creative visualization and flunk it because of a yearning disability?

5. Have you been so frustrated lately that you've started carrying around a disappointment book?

6. While other children had imaginary friends, did you have imaginary enemies?

7. When you first heard people affirming, "The universe totally supports me," did you consider suing the universe for nonsupport?

8. Are you convinced that life is a game of badminton, and you are the birdie?

9. When you became aware that we choose our own parents, did you become very excited because you realized that with the parents you got this time around, you'd get a first round draft choice next lifetime?

10. Have you discovered your inner child and now find he/she still has to be toilet trained?

0–2 "Yes" answers: If you had any more of a stable personality, you'd be Mr. Ed.

3–5 "Yes" answers: Your struts look good, but your shock absorbers are beginning to show some wear.

6–8 "Yes" answers: You're wanted in twelve emotional states for driving your karma recklessly.

More than 8 "Yes" answers: There's still hope, if you get a check-up from a competent metaphysician.

Swami Tells You How You Can Cure All Your Hang-ups Forever!

Are you hung up on being hung up on? Or do you hang others up because of your own hang-ups? They say these are times of scarcity, but believe me, if there's one thing we have plenty of, it's hang-ups. Particularly telephone hang-ups. According to a recent telephone poll, 65 percent of the people in this country are hung up about leaving messages on telephone answering machines. And 83 percent of the people who own these stupid machines are hung up about people hanging up on them! A lot of people, when you ask them why they don't leave messages, say they feel foolish talking to a machine. Now isn't that ridiculous? If you were being foolish, do you think a machine would actually know the difference? Or care? So I tell them only a *fool* would feel foolish talking to a machine! Besides, if they hated to talk into machines that much, why would they be using the telephone in the first place?

And the other kind of people, those with answering machines. Boy, these are some hung-up people. And you know, the more hung up they are, the more they get hung up on. And the more they get hung up on, the more hung up they get about getting hung up on. See, these are the people who have phone machines because they are afraid they're going to miss something. So when these people come home and hear those dialtones that tell them five people called without leaving messages, their egos get as squashed as if they'd been flattened by an esteem roller.

Swami Answers Your Questions About Hang-ups

Dear Swami:
How can I absolutely insure that people will leave a message on my answering machine?

Dick Tafone,
Hoboken, New Jersey

Dear Dick:

It's simple. Just tell them on your taped message that you'll send them $50 if they leave their name and number. And you'll find them calling back again and again and again. In fact, their friends will call too. And they'll keep calling back as long as you can afford it.

★

Dear Swami:

I got a hang-up. See, I'm hung up on this guy but I'm not sure if he's hung up on me. Sometimes I come home and there are some hang-ups on my machine and I wonder, did he hang up on me? Or am I just hanging myself up? I know I shouldn't get hung up on getting hung up on, but I can't help it—I'm hung up on him. Can you help me, Swami?

Ann Sadat,
Detroit, Michigan

Dear Ann:

No, I don't think so.

★

Dear Swami:

I've been trying to reach you for weeks. I desperately need your help! Every time I call, I seem to get this machine. Please help me!

Nora Ply,
San Jose, California

Thank you for calling Swami Beyondananda. The Swami is not in right now, but if you leave your name and number at the beep, he will be glad to get back to you real soon.

So if you've got a charge about telephone answering machines, call the Swami now and learn how you can reverse the charges!

Tantrum Yoga: The Latest Rage on the Path to Ire Consciousness

People ask me what it's like to be a higher being and I can tell right away they don't get it. Listen, the food that I eat is the same that you eat (except I put ketchup on everything). I put my pants on the usual way, one leg at a time. And just like you, I get mad. Plenty mad! I mean *furious*. The only difference is, I've learned to put my rage to work for me through daily practice of Tantrum Yoga. And I create enough energy to heat my ashram and several adjoining buildings.

See, a lot of people get angry. Well, that's great. Except they feel ashamed of their anger, and they feel angry at themselves for getting angry. Which makes them even angrier. Finally, they stub their toe on something just to release all the steam. Blam! They've shot their wad, and what do they have to show for it? Energy splattered all over the place—and a sore toe. So I say, don't hide your anger like a big baby. ACT YOUR RAGE!

THE FOUR BASIC POSTURES OF TANTRUM YOGA

Posture One: The King Kong.

When you experience the first twinges of anger or frustration, adopt the King Kong pose. Hunch your shoulders, clench your fists and make snorting noises. Imagine the problems that are disturbing you to be World War I airplanes, and flail at them with futile abandon.

Posture Two: The Funky King Kong.

When you've worked yourself into a tizzy (if you can't find a tizzy, a fret will do), begin to stomp around the room grunting loudly, and bring your arms up and down in the King Kong mudra (fists in front of chest, thumbs up). Now imagine your problems as hysterical New Yorkers being squished under your feet. If your problem *is* hysterical New Yorkers, all the better.

Posture Three: The Frantic Tantrum Mantra.

Lie on your back, flail your arms and shout the mantra, "NO-O-O-O-O!" at the top of your lungs. The vibrational quality of the word "No" really helps to clear the air, not to mention the entire neighborhood. When you feel you are about to collapse with exhaustion, tighten all your muscles and *hold your breath.* This is an ancient Hindu practice, and it works! How do you think Krishna got to be blue?

Posture Four: The Volcano.

Here's where you channel all that energy. Still holding your breath, get into a seated pose, stick your mouth straight up and exhale with a roar. You will feel like an erupting volcano. (To curb actual lava flow, it is advisable not to eat for three hours before performing tantrum yoga.) This fourth posture is also known as the "breath of fire" and is an excellent way to find out if your smoke alarm works.

Swami Answers Your Questions About Tantrum Yoga

Dear Swami:
  I've tried your Tantrum Yoga techniques and for the life of me, I just can't get angry. It's making me furious! What can I do?

                                        Ira Zentit,
                                        Los Angeles, California

Dear Ira:

Whatever you do, don't get angry at yourself for not getting angry! The best way to bring anger to the surface is to try not to get angry.

★

Dear Swami:

I agree with Tantrum Yoga in principle, but I can't seem to get into the practice. I guess I feel it's not ladylike to express anger. Any ideas?

Tanya Hyde,
Chattanooga, Tennessee

Dear Tanya:

Now I know in the past women have been taught not to disclose their rage. Listen, I have news for you—your rage shows anyway! So don't lie about your rage. Be proud of it. And people will say, "You know, she's not bad considering her rage—in fact, she's a raving beauty!"

★

Dear Swami,

Sometimes I'm in a fit of rage and begin doing Tantrum Yoga, but the anger wears off in the middle of the process. So my question is, should I make myself feel angry to complete the process or should I just let it go?

Hyman Dignant,
University City, Missouri

Dear Hyman,

Hey—if the fit wears, shoo it.

Yes, sign up for Tantrum Yoga now—it's guaranteed to be a pique experience.

Handle the Past

The past would be okay if it would just stay back there in our old photo albums where it belongs. But unfortunately, it follows us. For each of the positive photos we've kept, there's a negative which we've held on to as well. And since most of us hate to throw anything away, we still take these negatives with us wherever we go—even when we no longer need them to develop.

The good news is, there is a powerful technique for letting bygones be bygones (or, if you're into the Indian scene, letting Baghwans be Baghwans), and it is called Reburping.

REBURPING

It is true that our earliest experiences have a tremendous impact on us. In fact, some people have been so impacted that they can never let anything go. Why do we have so many traumas dating back to our infancy? The answer is alimentary. The truth is, most of our problems stem from having intestinal gas as little babies and not being able to get rid of it. This condition is called "Burp Trauma." That is when we sit around waiting passively for someone to burp us. And it is a pity we cannot accomplish anything all because we have no burp-us in life.

You may think of this as just a passing difficulty, but in truth it is something that will come up repeatedly unless released once and for all. Fortunately, there are techniques like Reburping and Primal Belch Therapy which teach you to let these painful experiences flow through you, so to speak, instead of holding them in. Developed by the great Native

American medicine man Broken Wind, reburping maintains that the release of gas is the most natural thing in the world—in fact it is our burp-right. Or, as reburpers say, "To air is human."

Just as each of us must choose his or her own path, so we choose the path of release as well—what reburpers call "the high road" and "the low road." While the high road is more socially acceptable in Western society, the low road is more fun to watch in a hot tub. Reburpers also believe in working with the mind, because hot air rises and often settles in the brain. "That is why there are so many airheads," says Broken Wind. "But once they release their burp trauma, they'll be able to become solid citizens without losing their lightness—and they'll discover for themselves the underlying principle of reburping: 'Life is a gas!'"

Give Yourself an Esteem Bath Daily

Just about every spiritual master nowadays tells us we're supposed to love ourselves, but few of us actually know how to do this. That's because our parents never taught us any of the positions. You see, from the time we are little being-sprouts we are told that we are good or bad, depending what we do. Let's face it, most love is given conditionally. In fact, it's so hard to find unconditional love nowadays that I include it as a premium with every book or tape I sell. That is right. If you buy a Swami Beyondananda book or tape, I promise to love you unconditionally!

But what if you can't get to a store and you need that unconditional love *right now*? Well, I've got some good news. You can be your own esteem generator! Feel like you got the cold shoulder? Try some esteem heat. Just stand in front of a mirror, look yourself in the I, and give yourself an esteem bath. Immerse yourself in good feelings, shower yourself with adulation, bathe yourself in love. Do this every day, and you will always leave your house under a full head of esteem.

And if you look at yourself in the mirror and you are not satisfied with the shape you're in, that is okay too, because our thoughts shape our lives. So here are some fresh thoughts to dab on after your esteem bath which will help you get in shape:

Appreciate yourself. If you are feeling worthless, that is great, because it means you've already bottomed out. So take stock of yourself. In fact, take as much stock as you can, because the price will never be better. You can go public later. Invest in yourself by appreciating yourself. Because the more you appreciate yourself, the more your Self will appreciate.

Stop criticizing yourself. Self-criticism is bad for your health. It builds up and builds up until you reach what is called a critical mass—and before you know it, you're on the critical list. So whatever it is you feel the urge to criticize yourself about, turn it into an appreciation of a positive trait. If you must acknowledge a failure, give yourself credit (even if your creditors won't). You say your third business venture in two years just went blooey? Don't say, "I'm a failure when it comes to being successful." Turn it around by saying, "I am tremendously successful at failing." That way, you can't lose! And whatever you do, don't criticize yourself for being self-critical.

Don't criticize others, either. Two things that do the most to damage our personal relationships are judgment and blame. I think people who judge are terrible—and those who blame are the cause of all the world's problems. Remember, it is we who create our own reality (even though a lot of reality is now made in Taiwan, because of the cheaper labor). So don't tell another human being, "You are an inconsiderate jerk." Take responsibility for what you have attracted. Say, "I take full responsibility for attracting an inconsiderate jerk like you into my life."

Practice reverse paranoia. When you see people whispering to each other at the next table at a restaurant, are you convinced they are whispering about you? They are, you know. They are saying, "Get a load of that beautiful beaming beacon of God-light over at that next table!" Even if they aren't whispering that at all, it sure feels good to imagine they are. Yes, even as you read this, the universe is plotting to make you utterly happy, healthy and successful. *And there isn't a thing you can do about it!*

Make friends with your inner child. Your inner child is a terrific kid, but most of us are so busy being adults that we leave our inner child at home whenever we go anywhere— and we don't even bother to get a babysitter. So I suggest you start taking your inner child out to the park, to the movies, to the zoo. And if you feel blocked, ask your inner child for help. Your inner child loves to play with blocks!

Make sure you laugh at least once a day. Laughter opens you up to let life's experiences flow through you. If you are not laughing regularly, you may be suffering from humorrhoids—hardened attitudes which may actually lower your laugh expectancy. So I suggest taking a laughsitive daily—about one milidangerfield should be sufficient—and that should restore regular-hilarity.

What to Do if Things Get too Good

Emotion sickness has its ups as well as downs, my children, and this can be a major source of difficulties, mainly because society at large is not used to such unbridled euphoria. Some of the dangers are as follows:

Alienation of friends and family. Let's face it. Normal folks have a hard time being around people who are truly ecstatic about everyday, mundane things. Even though TV commercials tell you to do your dishes with Joy, when we start swooning and exclaiming that we *see God* washing the dishes, that's a little hard to believe. (Everyone knows that God has a dishwasher.) Let's face it. When we ourselves are not feeling all that great, seeing someone else in the throes of euphoria makes us want to—well, throe up.

Trouble with the authorities. People who seem unusually happy come under suspicion for drug use, particularly now that there are drugs which leave no trace in the body. One of these substances, made popular by Oliver North, is called "deniasin." Deniasin dissolves guilt in minutes and leaves no unpleasant aftertaste—except in those who *do not* swallow it.

Actual physical danger. Not everybody loves a clown and even though popular wisdom says, "A mime is a terrible thing to waste," some folks react violently to smiling faces. New York City, for example, has recently reinstated mandatory prison sentences for painting smile faces on subway cars.

Given all of these problems with uncontrollable happiness, it's a good thing I have developed a training to make sure your feet are still mired in some earthly mud even if you're being a soar-head:

FEELING TOO GOOD LATELY?

- Do you suffer from unexplained feelings of euphoria?
- Are you entirely too pleased with the way you look?
- Are you feeling downright lovable and happy?
- Are you sick and tired of people you don't even know liking you for no apparent reason?

Well, my friends, if your answer to any of these is yes, then you need Swami Beyondananda's new seminar, Now on cassette tape: *Guilt: Where To Get It, How To Keep It.*

Says the Swami: "Look at you! You ought to be ashamed of yourselves! We have become a nation of fun-loving pleasure-seekers who forget just how bad things are, or could be. We are quickly losing touch with the greatest motivating force in the world—GUILT! Have you ever stopped to think where we'd be without guilt? Jewish mothers would all leave home en masse and become party girls down in Bimini. Charities would need charity to support *themselves.* And love would *really* mean never having to say you're sorry. Why, we'd be barely civilized."

Yes, now achieving Guilt Awareness can be as easy as putting on a headset. Now you can feel bad about everything that's wrong with the world and never leave the comfort of your easy chair. Listen as Swami helps you:

- Reclaim old guilt and create new.
- Learn the mantra that has helped people feel guilty down through the ages: "Oy."
- Learn the real reasons why you are no good and should feel rotten.

. Tap into the cosmic well of misery that's in us all.

Here's what our satisfyingly distressed listeners have to say:

> "Oy, do I feel guilty!"
>   —J.Y., Ozone Park, N.Y.

> "Never in my life have I felt so abjectly terrible. Thank you, Swami, for letting me see things as they really are."
>   —L.K., Des Plaines, Ill.

> "Feeling bad sure takes a lot of work, but boy is it worth it!"
>   —R.J.L., Tampa, Fla.

So act now! There's no need to feel contented or satisfied any longer. Send us $10.95 today and Swami will send you his new cassette, "Happiness Can't Last." Or send us a dollar less, and feel *really* guilty!

Swami Beyondananda Answers All Your Questions About Looking Out for Number Two

Dear Swami:
I have a real problem. I am plagued by phobias. You name it, I've got it: claustrophobia, agoraphobia, xenophobia. Not only am I afraid of the dark, but the light scares me as well because I'm afraid of my own shadow. Not a week goes by without my developing some new phobia. In fact, the whole time I was writing this letter I was gripped by swamiscript-ophobia, or fear of writing letters to swamis. Please help me!
>   *Too scared to tell you my name,*
>   *Chicago, Illinois*

Dear Scared:

Sounds like you have a serious mental problem. But that's easy to fix because, after all, mental problems are all in your mind! If you're so good at developing phobias, I suggest you develop a fear of phobias. Do this, and I guarantee you'll be too afraid to be fearful anymore.

★

Dear Swami:

I've been having financial problems lately, so much so that I've been unable to pay my rent. I found this very upsetting until I decided to seek spiritual counsel. I opened up my "Course In Miracles," and the first thing I read was, "You are not upset for the reason you think." That was immensely comforting to me. My question is, what do I tell the landlord?
Max Stout,
Boulder, Colorado

Dear Max:

How about, "You're not upset for the reason you think"?

★

Dear Swami:

I'd like to have more alone time. What do you suggest?
Chuck Itall,
Beaverton, Oregon

Dear Chuck:

Lots of garlic.

★

Dear Swami:

I know you are an expert on blockages, so tell me—is bran the only answer?

Rich D. Zertz,
Roslyn, Long Island

Dear Rich:

You will be happy to know that I am coming out with a new product that is not only natural, but actually dates back to Biblical times. It is called Moses Brand Laxative, and it comes in two very large tablets. On the package is a picture of Moses looking out into the desert. He doesn't know exactly where the children of Israel are bound, only that they *will* be bound something terrible, what with eating nothing but matzoh for the next 40 years. His hand is raised to the skies and he is imploring, "Let my people go!"

★

Dear Swami:

I've been putting off writing this letter for months. Tell me, is there any cure for procrastination?

Ho Lai Minh,
Seattle, Washington

Dear Ho:

Of course there is. Next time you get the urge to procrastinate—put it off.

★

Dear Swami:

Now that I've done some past-life work, I feel ashamed about all of those things I did that I shouldn't have done— and all the things I didn't do that I should have. I'm plagued by regrets. Can you help me?

Kenya Diggett,
Washington, D.C.

Dear Kenya:

It sounds like you're suffering from "rebirth trauma." Fortunately, there is now a way to handle all your past-life regrets—through "past-life regretsion." Through a technique in time travel I call "Be There Now," you can go back and relive any of your lives any way you want to—and still be back in time to watch the six o'clock news. Not only will fixing up your past lives enhance their resale value, but with your past complete you can begin looking ahead—and fixing up your future lives as well.

★

Dear Swami:
  What is the quickest route to enlightenment?

Doris Sopen,
Madison, Wisconsin

Dear Doris:
  The quickest route to enlightenment used to be Route 66. But now it's a lot quicker to get on I–40, although I suggest a detour in Arizona just so you can get a sense of Yuma. If you're not driving, let me suggest a new training I have developed. Swami Beyondananda's Speed Suffering Course is the fastest route to enlightenment. Consider it a consolidation loan for all your karmic debts. Cram eons worth of suffering into one miserable week! You will hate it! But when it's over, your dues are paid forever and you can go to the beach.

★

Dear Swami:
  I've been told that all I need to do to achieve happiness is give up my attachment to money. What do you suggest I do?

I.D. Klein,
Rock Hill, South Carolina

Dear I. D.:
  Don't do a thing until I get there.

☆
PART THREE
The Miracle of
Tell-A-Vision

Do you realize that the most powerful tool we have for manifesting our heart's desire is Tell-A-Vision? No, I'm not talking about "Moonlighting" or "Die-Nasty" or the six o'clock news. I'm talking about you tell a vision to me, I tell a vision to you. That way, everybody becomes their own channel. So don't always assume that father knows best, and for goodness sake don't leave it to Beaver. Forget about your old taped programs. In the coming good years, we are going back to live broadcasting.

You see, each of us is on the planet for a very important reason—and Tell-A-Vision helps us find our special gift. The first thing you must do is turn on your power. Good. Now what do you see? You may have to change channels for a while, but if you just keep tuning in, you'll get the picture. Once you have a vision of what you would love to be doing, tell everyone you know. This will put it out over the airwaves, so to speak, and who knows? You may be asked to do a pilot, or even a miniseries. Don't worry about ratings. As long as *you* are turned on, people will tune into you.

How Swami Discovered His Special Gift

As a young child growing up in Oklahoma, I discovered at an early age that I had a mystical bent. My parents took me to several chiropractors who said that I'd outgrow it, but it just became more pronounced. Like in class. You know how children fall asleep in class and unobtrusively put their heads down on their desks? When I fell asleep, I would float to the top of the room. The teacher would yell something at me— and that would be my downfall. When they would drag me to the principal's office, I would patiently explain that I was following my higher self. My parents tried everything— including grounding me—but I continued to get high in class on a regular basis.

My father was wise enough to know that this was no simple problem. He knew of a great Native American medicine man living nearby, and he took me to see him. The medicine man dubbed me "High Rise" and told my father he'd be responsible for helping me use my gift wisely.

Thus began my apprenticeship with the great Indian shaman, Broken Wind. It was with Broken Wind that I first learned to converse with the trees, the streams, the rocks, and the clouds. Now at first, I really didn't know what to talk about. I mean, the weather is a good topic to start with— particularly with clouds—but after a while the conversation falls flat and you sit around feeling very uncomfortable. I remember going on and on to some maple tree I had just met, about the girls I liked at school and baseball and the latest Jerry Lewis movie, when I heard the loud creaking of a large branch, which sounded a lot like a yawn. "Am I boring you?" I asked the tree.

"Nah," said the tree. "The guys who take my sap for syrup in the springtime—now *they* bore me!"

"Oh, yes," said Broken Wind when I relayed the quip to him. "All those philosophers who write books about the nature of Intelligence would be better off studying the intelligence of Nature instead. After all, without trees there'd *be* no books."

At that point, Broken Wind told me it was time for my Tell-A-Vision Quest. He led me through the woods to a house that looked like everyone's 1950's suburban dream home— aluminum siding and all. "This," he announced, "is your No-Sweat Lodge. Whatever you want, no sweat. It's yours. TV, ice cream, pizza. You will be required to stay here for five days."

"Hey, no sweat," I said.

And for the first day and a half, it was terrific. All the "Twilight Zone" and "I Love Lucy" I could handle, no one to tell me to do chores or homework or go to bed. But by late in the second day, I began to feel a little sick—probably due to the chocolate cake I had eaten while watching "Sea Hunt." That was okay. A couple of slabs of pizza and a large Pepsi should balance things out, I figured. By the third day, my stomach was so distended I couldn't cross my legs. So I sat like Buddha in front of the tube (in what I later discovered was the Bloatus pose) and watched game show after game show.

By the end of the third day I was so bored and exhausted from digestion that I couldn't stand it any longer. I called for Broken Wind and told him I had had enough. "You have two more days to go," he replied sternly. "Sure, being a great warrior requires hardship, but you must learn to take the good as well as the bad. Now what would you like on that pizza?"

Those last two days were like a hazy dream to me. Maybe it was the mushrooms on those pizzas, but I hallucinated constantly. When I finally awoke, the TV was off and my stomach was almost back to its normal size and shape. Broken Wind sat nearby, a faint smile on his face. "Good work, High Rise. You have passed the first test of being a warrior—satiation. You have been sated beyond your wildest imagination, and now know that being sated is not all that satisfying. And you are much stronger now because you will never again be tempted by sat'n."

I suddenly felt a wave of nausea, and I rushed to the bathroom, where I expelled five days worth of pizza, chocolate cake, westerns, and situation comedies (those reruns are never as good the second time).

When I returned, Broken Wind said, "It is good. We are taught to fill ourselves with things so that we feel full. But being filled full isn't necessarily fulfillment. Now that you are empty you are ready to be fulfilled."

He was right. The emptiness I now felt was more fulfilling than any full feeling I'd ever had.

"And now," Broken Wind said to me, "it is time for the second part of your Tell-A-Vision Quest. This is where you learn to produce your own program. You must get in touch with the Director of Programming and find out what most needs to be broadcast at this time."

"How do I do that?" I asked.

"By tuning in to all the major channels, and by listening with your Third Ear."

"My Third Ear? What's that?"

"That is when you turn off the picture and turn up the sound. Listen carefully enough, and you will create your own picture. Listen to Nature—trees, plants, animals, streams, desert, rocks. You will then go into the woods. There you will meet your Power Animal, who will help you tell your vision. Return to me within a week, and we will see if you have passed the test."

So I spent the next week listening to nature like I had never listened before. The chattering squirrels, the babbling brooks, the whistling wind, the whispering pines. I went to the zoo that week and stood for hours in front of the apes. What at first seemed to me aimless chattering began sounding like sweet music. In fact, it reminded me of my favorite Christmas choir—the Hairy Simian Chorale. I even listened to the rocks, who were stony silent. I decided to call their bluff, but the bluff never answered.

My next stop was the woods, and I realized it was here that my Tell-A-Vision quest would culminate. By now, I had become so auditorily sensitive that sound became a part of everything I did. All the training had given me a sound body and a sound mind. And I soon drifted into a sound sleep.

I was awakened by a slow clop of hooves. I looked up to see a horse with a sardonic expression on his face. "Uh, hullo," the horse said.

I sat up with a start. "You're talking!" I said.

"Well, it might look that way," the horse replied, "but actually God has taken up ventriloquism. Pretty good, huh?"

I had to admit that I hadn't noticed His lips move.

"You see," the horse continued, "with all the influence

television is having nowadays, the Creator decided that it was time to give Nature a voice on TV. And I was chosen as the channel."

"Wait a minute," I said. "I *thought* you looked familiar. You're Mr. Ed!" The horse curled his upper lip in a toothy grin. "Are you my Power Animal?"

The horse nodded affirmatively and said, "I have been sent here to help you make the switch from television to Tell-A-Vision. See, nowadays people turn on the tube hoping the tube will turn *them* on. But in the very near future, we will each become our own programming director. So now let's play *This Is Your Life*. Only instead of looking at your past, let's tune in to your future. To see this picture, you must close your eyes."

I closed my eyes, and gradually a picture appeared on my inner screen. It took me a couple of minutes to get the picture just right (they never tell you how to adjust the vertical in those creative visualization classes), but soon I could see myself leading what seemed to be a religious service—and the theme was obviously fun and laughter. Around my neck, I wore a flexible rubber likeness of a smiling Bullwinkle Moose, his arms outstretched in joy. This symbol was the subject of my sermon, or "shtick," as we called it. I told the assembled that it was called a "Moosafix," and just the sight of it is enough to convert disbelievers to FUNdamentalism. The outstretched arms of the Moosafix reminds us that the only kind of arms race worth winning is to see how many of our fellow human beings we can hug in a lifetime.

I then announced that it was time for the "Uncritical Mass," a communion where people took the FUNdamentalists' favorite spiritual foods—Snickers and Chuckles. After that special ceremony the children returned from Funday School, and to the delight of everyone, acted out "Who's On

First" and several Far Side cartoons. A collection plate was passed, and people threw in cartoons, joke books, and comedy tapes to be donated to the humorless. And then the service was over, with the congregation responding "Th-th-th-th-that's all folks!" instead of "amen."

The picture faded, and I slowly returned to my spot in the woods. Mr. Ed was still there, and he seemed to sense that I had had a profound religious experience. "Will that wonderful vision really come true?" I asked.

He nodded. "If it can be imagined, it's conceivable. What you see is what you get, because after all we are each a figment of our own imagination." With this, Mr. Ed yawned and said, "Well, I think my job here is done. I'm gonna go grab me a beer."

"Horses drink beer?" I asked.

"Draft horses do," he winked, and trotted on down the road.

A week later I returned for the Test. "So, young High Rise, what did nature have to say about your purpose?"

"Well," I answered, "I have learned it is my purpose to be in harmony with All Things. I know how we humans always want to sing lead, but that is not always appropriate. There are millions of voices, and all are beautiful. There's a time for the high parts, there's even a time to follow our bass instincts. Each of us is an instrument with our own tune to play. And we all can be great conductors, provided we get rid of our resistance."

He nodded. "And how do you plan to use *your* special gift, your ability to levitate?" he asked.

I thought for a moment. "Well, I will teach levity. My program will be a situation comedy—because through laughter, we can rise to any situation. Since in truth we are all light, why not lighten up?"

"You have passed the test," he said, "and your work with me is finished. You will meet many great teachers on your journey, and you will achieve the coveted black belt in Three Stooges Self-Defense. You will become a famous Comic-kaze warrior. Go now to your people and increase their laugh expectancy. May the Farce be with you."

Swami's Tell-A-Vision Meditation For Finding Your Special Gift

What is *your* special gift? Now, please don't tell me you don't have one, because that is not true. Each of us, when we come down the chute, is given a special gift, *just for entering!* So *you are already a winner!* That's right. This gift is pre-programmed, although we don't usually get it immediately. No, we must claim it at some future time. And this is how we redeem ourselves. The following meditation will insure your redemption:

To begin this meditation, sit quietly in your favorite TV easy chair. If you haven't got an easy chair, that is probably your major problem right there. Go buy one, and relax! Now sitting in your chair, imagine the TV screen in front of you. When you turn on the power, a wise spiritual guide will appear on the screen. His name is TV Guide and he will help you tune into your program. I say he, but it could be a she as well. In fact, your TV Guide can take any form you like, from Ed McMahon to Vanna White to Bugs Bunny. When your TV Guide has fully materialized, he or she will say to you, "Good evening and welcome to *What's My Lifetime?* We've got some great entertainment lined up for you—and also some

fabulous prizes. And this is a show where everybody partici-
pates, okay? Good. Now, in a minute I'm going to ask you to
come up here and create your own program with the help of
our *What's My Lifetime?* panel. Yes, you produce this program, you direct it, you act in it. The Universe is the Sponsor,
and believe me, no matter what your ratings are, the Sponsor
will never cancel your show. Only you can do that.

"Now, your show can be anything you want: drama, situation comedy, game show, news, talk show, soap opera, po-
lice drama, or even cartoons. And of course, you can always
choose a new format when you're tired of the old one. Right
now, I'd like you to whisper your secret heart's desire to me
and we'll let the studio audience and the folks at home know
just what you think this lifetime is all about."

(You whisper your secret heart's desire. The studio audience and the folks at home now know what it is. You have
engaged your Tell-A-Vision transmitter, and you now have
thousands and thousands of fans cheering for you.)

"Very good. Now, of course, coming up with an idea for a
'Special' and actually producing it are two different things.
That's where our *What's My Lifetime?* panel of experts
comes in. They represent the Major Channels and with their
questions they'll help you make sure your program fits with
their Format.

"So here to ask the first question, representing Channeled
Entities, that 50,000-year-old funnyman, back from a fabu-
lously successful disappearance at the Lemuria Hilton,
please welcome—Bizarris!" (Applause.)

BIZARRIS: "Thank you, Beings, thank you. A funny thing, as it
were, happened to me on the way to the studio tonight. A man
came up to me and said, 'Can you please help me? I haven't had
that which is called a bite in three days.' I replied, 'I'd love to help

you, but disembodied entities have no teeth.' (Laughter) Indeed! But seriously—and I mean that—does this program you are visioning, does it really excite you? Does it make you feel absolutely enthused and exhilarated? Because if you want your karma to go full speed ahead, Embodied One, your exhilarator pedal has to work!"

(Answer his question.)

TV GUIDE: *"Thanks, Bizarris. And now, to represent those really far out folks from across the galaxy, please welcome our favorite space cadet, Miss Gracie Alien. (Applause.) Gracie, I understand you were hosting the Intergalactic Space Craft Show. What's your favorite space craft?"*

GRACIE ALIEN: "Oh, that would have to be the Laser Macrame from Andromeda. Anyway, my question has to do with the importance of planning any venture. I mean, we extra-terrestials have been visiting Earth for centuries now, and we wouldn't dream of coming without reservations. And if you've seen Earth lately, you'd have reservations about coming, too. So my question is, are you willing to plan your program as carefully as if you were planning a journey into space? Because you know what they say—if you wanna be a star you gotta planet."

(Answer her question.)

TV GUIDE: *"Wonderful, Gracie. Planning is indeed important— with a daily plan-it, anyone can be a Superbeing. And now to represent our cousins from the animal realm, let's welcome that star of the new musical, A Taurus Line, Mr. Bo Vine! (Applause.) Bo, how did you get started in movies?"*

BO VINE: "Well, like many actors, my 'overnight success' came only after a long struggle. I started out doing summer stock. For years, I'd show up for cattle call after cattle call and finally landed some bit parts in a couple of cowboy flicks—strictly beefcake. I was just another face in the herd until one day a talent scout noticed my dairy-air, exclaimed 'Holy Cow!'—and here I am."

TV GUIDE: *"And what is your question for our* What's My Lifetime? *contestant?"*

BO VINE: "You know, we animals have a saying: 'If it feels good, do it.' I mean, we're not much for intellectualizing and we'd never make it in college (except maybe as party animals). Give me a sweet, brown-eyed cow and some good grass and I'll be satisfied. So my question is, when you play your program on your internal VCR, does it feel good? You humans have plenty of animal in you, and pleasure makes a difference—so if you aren't enjoying a particular program, you're sure to switch channels at your first commercial break."

(Answer his question.)

TV GUIDE: *"And that's no bull, either. Thank you, Bo Vine. You know, we're often asked whether the guests on this show are plants. They're not, but one of our panelists is. Please welcome our next panelist, Miss Rhoda Dendron!" (Applause.)*

RHODA DENDRON: "Thank you. You know, I've been studying people for many years—in fact, I used to lead human nature walks in New York City. And a lot of people get really arrogant about nature—like the Earth is beneath them or something. And it had better be, at least as long as they're on the physical plane. So my question is this: Is your program in harmony with nature? Because if it is, then it will no longer feel like a 'jungle' out there—it will be a garden."

(You answer.)

TV GUIDE: *"Thank you, Rhoda. I admit I've never been all that fond of plants, but what can I say. I've definitely taken a lichen to you. (Laughter sign flashed to audience.) Moving right along, I'd like to introduce our next panelist, a solid guy from the mineral realm, the world-reknowned boxer-turned-comedian—or is it comedian-turned-boxer—please welcome Mr. Rocky Crystal! (Applause.) Rocky, it must be hard being both a boxer and a comedian. Do you ever get mixed up?"*

ROCKY CRYSTAL: "Hey, absolutely! Sometimes I get killed out there doing comedy, and sometimes my boxing is a joke. But one thing is true in both roles—you gotta be as grounded as a rock, and as clear as a crystal. And that's my question: Is your program firmly grounded in reality, and is your vision crystal clear? Because that's what separates the diamond from the molten masses who live in igneous."

(You answer.)

TV GUIDE: *"My sediments exactly, Rocky. And now it's time to introduce our final panelist, one who represents the realm of technology. Please welcome that master of the Holy Integrated Circuit, Baba ROM Dos. (Applause.) ROM Dos, let me ask you a personal question. How does it feel to be completely man-made?"*

ROM DOS: "Probably not a lot different than being human. You see, all of us are man-made in a sense. Just as you humans program us computers, so you program your own inner computer. I am a firm believer in GIGO—Greatness In, Greatness Out. So my question is, are you willing to program yourself with only thoughts that will further your greatness? Because if you do this, no power surge or crash will be able to erase your Program."

(You answer.)

TV GUIDE: *"Thank you, ROM Dos. You know, I knew you were a more spiritual computer when I looked on your screen and instead of a cursor, you had a blessor.*

"Okay. You've had a chance to meet our distinguished panelists representing the Major Channels. You've answered all their questions, and if you told the Truth, the Consequences will be magnificent. And along with the Grand Prize—being the star of your own Tell-A-Vision Program—we have another gift to take with you on your journey."

(TV Guide's hand opens, and you see a small, silvery gleaming object.)

"As a special gift for being a part of the show, here's a powerful little tool to keep you in tune—your Perfect Pitchpipe to make sure you're always in harmony. This silver beauty is an exact replica of the one God uses to tune up the Universe every hundred million years—or sixty-thousand lightyears, whichever comes first. Next time life plays a clunker, don't despair. Blow a note on this. You'll get that perfect pitch—and when you do, you'll smack it for a home run. And now let's have a big hand for our Contestant."

(A huge hand emerges from behind stage and gently lifts you in the air. You feel calm and at ease.)

TV GUIDE: *"And now a word from our Sponsor, All States Insurance. Yes, whatever karma you're driving, you're in good hands with All States. And don't worry, you'll never be dropped. The Universe hasn't made any errors for the past million or so seasons. We're just about out of time, but there should be more coming any minute. Goodnight and thank you for playing* What's My Lifetime? *May your Program run indefinitely and may you enjoy reruns of the best shows forevermore."*

LESSON 9: TUNING IN TO THE MAJOR CHANNELS

Once you have had the experience of Tell-A-Vision, you will have an idea of why you have incarnated at this time. Now, I am a firm believer in reincarnation, although that has not always been the case. In several of my previous lives, I have been quite skeptical about reincarnation. But now I am what they call born again, born again, born again, born again Krishna. And I believe in the Born Again Krishna credo, which is, "You only go around 60 million times, so grab the gusto!" And of course reincarnation makes sense. After all, if we are expected to recycle, why shouldn't God? Anyway, it is we who choose our Tell-A-Vision Program long before the new season begins. And the universe had provided us with several Major Channels to help us improve our programming and offer us guidance in reaching our true TV station in life.

DISEMBODIED ENTITIES

Some of the most talked-about channels for information— particularly in recent years—are disembodied entities from other dimensions. Believe me, *everyone* is channeling nowadays. In fact, the channels are all taken up and I've had to go on cable. Having said that, let me admit that everything in this book is channeled—so if you don't like it, it's not my fault.

These disembodied beings are having a difficult time lately. You see, in between lifetimes it is a lot like being unemployed. You can collect disembodiment insurance for about thirteen weeks, then you have to find a body. Which is not that easy to do nowadays, particularly with so many of us on the earth plane practicing safe sex. Sure, there are some openings among some of the lower vibrational creatures, but truthfully, after you've gone around a couple of times as a squirrel, it loses its charm.

These disembodied beings are lined up twenty deep for reincarnation, and I feel bad for them. They have closets full of clothes, and nothing to wear them on. And it is an esteem issue as well. They feel like "no bodies." Besides, certain activities simply require a physical form. I don't care how good your personality is, if you don't have a body, no one is going to ask you to the dance.

So here they are, these disembodied beings, looking for some body to call their own. And if they can't be reborn into one, then, by Ramtha, they'll find another way. Meanwhile, some of those beings on Earth who don't want the muss and fuss of having children are learning to bring beings in through other channels. Channeling disembodied entities beats childbirth and toilet training and PTA meetings and punk haircuts. And if you don't like the static you are receiving, you can always change the channel.

So how do these channeled entities get into bodies nowadays? Well, there are a lot of us who, through meditation and other spiritual exercises, are becoming more sensitive to astral goings on. Years ago, my own guru, Harry Cohen

Baba, used to insist I was a medium. (With all the Soul Food they serve on those higher planes, by now I must be a large.) I must admit I haven't had much luck channeling entities, although I have channeled a few nonentities. I seem to get composite personalities, like Cayce Stengel. He's a brilliant healer, except you can't understand a word he says.

But there are pitfalls to channeling, I must tell you. First of all, basic Universal Law says, "One soul per body, please." And that makes sense. Being in a body is difficult enough without having someone else in there with you whose "Things To Do" list is nothing like your own. But it's a hard law to enforce. I mean, there are a lot of bodies cruising around out there and really no way to know who is driving. Worse than that, some entity—who maybe hasn't driven a body around in seven centuries—takes your body on a joyride and says to itself, "You know this is so much fun, I think I'm gonna keep it!" And that is how a lot of karmas get stolen, my children.

There was an incident that happened recently with a Well-Known Channeled Entity—I won't name any names because I wouldn't want to get involved in either a Universal Lawsuit or interdimensional scandal. But anyway, this entity was cruising around in someone else's body and was stopped by the Higher State Patrol. He couldn't produce his occupancy permit and he was booked for possession.

And have you noticed that no being is ever satisfied? As hard as these disembodied entities are trying to get into bodies, those with bodies are trying to travel out of theirs! And that is dangerous, especially nowadays with all these walk-ins. You take a trip down to the astral Stop 'n' Shop for a package of Enlighten-Mints, and when you return you find your body is occupied—and the new owner has already redecorated. And there you are, stranded without a body—and no cash. (That is why I recommend that if you're traveling on the astral plane, get one of those Ascended MasterCards—and don't leave Om without it.)

I find it disturbing that someone can walk into your body while you are out of it, so to speak, and yet so many people are blithely accepting of this. I have walked by countless beauty parlors that have signs saying, "Walk-ins are welcome." My goodness! These walk-ins just got a new face. Let them enjoy it as it is!

Personally, I think channeling is fine. I disagree with those who feel these entities are a bunch of "no bodies" trying to muscle in on grow business. But I would issue this caution. As Harry Cohen Baba used to say, "Enlightenment is not a bureaucracy. So you don't *have* to go through channels."

HOW TO CHOOSE A DISEMBODIED ENTITY

Believe me, this planet and nearby dimensions are just crawling with disembodied beings trying to meet some body they can go home with. How do you know which entities are right for you? Well, right away you can rule out those who just want you for your body. You can recognize this type by their transparent opening lines ("Say, weren't you Queen Nefertiti in a previous lifetime?") and their overeagerness to connect ("If you *really* loved me, you'd share your body with me now"). You haven't much to learn from these entities— unless the Tell-A-Vision Program you've chosen is a soap opera.

The next category of disembodied entity is the "Doom Sayer." These are very popular because many people secretly hope the world will end—why, I don't really know. Maybe they've sat through this movie too many times before and are bored. Or maybe they see the end of the world as the one sure way to clear up the national debt. What-ever the reason, people will flock to hear some former re-porter for the Universal Enquirer predicting one disaster or another. Whether it's floods or droughts or asteroids or hemorrhoids—these beings get their thrills watching gullible mortals squirm with discomfort. But actually, these doom sayers serve a valuable function. They get people to wake up and pay attention.

Then there is the "Yentity," who is nothing more than an interdimensional busybody. These are the ones who tell you what Elvis is *really* up to nowadays (he and Buddy Holly have formed a new singing group called the "Foreverly Brothers") and also bear messages from your deceased Un-cle Fred or Cousin Chloe about life on The Other Side. My question to all the channeled Uncle Freds and the know-it-all Yentities that bring them forth is, "If you're so smart, why are you dead?"

Now there is one type of Channeled Entity that can be very beneficial. He (or she) is called the No Body Sattva. He is a fully realized being (actually, we're all realized—the dif-ference is that he realizes he's realized) who is himself pre-pared to merge with God, but has accepted the merger agreement contingent on the rest of us getting retrained before the merger takes place. And the retraining involves not so much merging, but emerging. In fact, this channeled entity has adopted emergency measures to help us emerge 'n' see who we really are. He's already seen it all and done it all over and over again. He knows all the world is a stage—just a stage we're passing through—so he has no acts to grind. Being in his presence is like being slurped by a happy puppy or cuddled by a teddy bear. You know you're in the presence of a No Body Sattva when you are bathed in unconditional love and feel as if everything in the world is your bath toy. Most importantly, the No Body Sattva will put all your worldly concerns in proper perspective by taking you beyond the material. "Why worry?" he says. "Reality is no matter."

EXTRA-TERRESTIALS

I have some very strong opinions about extra-terrestials. I say we already have enough terrestials. We don't need any extra. With all these Americans out of work, I think it's a crime to hire aliens. Now I know that some of those channels I just spoke about have predicted that at the right moment, beings from other galaxies will come and "beam up" the most righteous among us, and these chosen people will be whisked away to a better world. I think this is a nice fantasy, but personally I don't believe in flying sorcerers. I find it a little bit disturbing that so many people are placing all their faith in this Supreme Beam and meanwhile are sitting around passively waiting for their spaceship to come in. The way I figure it, if we *are* expecting company, we should at least straighten our place up a bit.

In fact, we Earthlings have a reputation around the solar system as very poor caretakers. With all the garbage we are spewing out into the solar system, we are bringing the property values way down. As some writers point out, these beings from outer space have been here before and left predictions which have been remarkably accurate. Perhaps you've heard of those ancient scrolls recently discovered in Egypt called the "Tut Sea Rolls"? Some of the misfortunes they predicted have already come to pass, including Heavy Metal Music, Machine-Harvested Tomatoes, and the dreaded Pestilence of Attorneys. But there is some good news as well. The Tut Sea Rolls also predict a great era of cooperation throughout the galaxy, where we all live together in peace and harmony. In fact, a huge festival promoting galactic unity has been planned for early in the next century. It will be called "Hands Across Uranus" and will feature many popular stars, including our own sun.

Another thing about these beings from outer space. They expect to learn a lot from us, particularly how to "turn on their heartlight." You see, these beings have a lot of wisdom and technical skills, but their feelings of love, joy, and playfulness are underdeveloped. They are a lot like that Mr. Spock character. This may be hard to believe, but in some regions of the universe gamboling is actually illegal. So our mission is to immerse these beings in Joy and Zest and Cheer—and when they leave our planet, their lives will be 40 percent brighter.

THE ANIMAL KINGDOM

Our cousins in the animal kingdom are great teachers of love and unconditional acceptance. That is why I have developed a powerful new training called *Teach Your Dog to Heal*.

That's right. No more need for expensive specialists, questionable drugs, or dangerous medical procedures. If it's healing energy you are looking for, you need only look as far as your backyard. My new booklet, "The Art of Sidekick Healing," reveals healing secrets doggedly guarded for ages.

No bones about it, unconditional love is the greatest healer. And who's better equipped to give unconditional love than person's best friend? Remember that medicine they used to advertise that was "nature's" spelled backward? Well, Dog is God spelled backward. So stop barking up the wrong tree. Shed those dogmatic beliefs about doctors, hospitals, even gurus. Forget about health insurance. Lasting health can be yours for the price of Gainesburgers.

How Dogs Can Heal

- It is a known scientific fact that the mere *sight* of a friendly dog induces the human body to produce puptides, chemicals that help the body fight disease and create a general feeling of well-being. This was proven in a now-famous experiment in the Swiss Alps, in which half of the rescue dogs were given casks of cognac to carry and the other half a placebo containing butterscotch Kool-Aid. Not only did those persons given Kool-Aid recover completely from exposure, but they suffered no hangover the next day.

- Studies show that dogs are 55 percent more effective than psychiatrists in treating mental illness, particularly in children. Dogs are experts at communicating love directly, they are born listeners, and even those dogs without formal training know when to use a firm paw or a gentle nuzzle.

- Dog owners have fewer heart attacks. It's a fact. That's because dogs get their people to go for walks instead of watching the 11 o'clock news. Says noted medical researcher Dr. Hugh Manitarian, "Not only is the walk much-needed exercise, but not watching the news results in 34 percent less stress!"

- And when it comes to skin disorders, dogs have the problem licked. That's right. The isolated ingredient in dog spittle (now sold over the counter as Love Potion K-9) has remarkable curative effects on skin problems of all kinds. In fact, the World Health Organization has enlisted the aid of a dedicated group of dogs, known as the Salivation Army, in their efforts to eliminate acne as a world health problem by 1998.

Here's what people around the country are saying about "Teach Your Dog To Heal":

Dear Swami:

Just a note to tell you how useful your book has been to us. We have converted the Humane Society here into a "Nuzzle For Health" clinic and we're getting people in here *before* they get sick. You know what they say: "An ounce of prevention is worth a pound of dogs."

L. Cound,
Hibbing, Minnesota

Dear Swami:

My dog, Dr. Spot, is world renowned as a healer of children. But is was not always so. Before Swami's training, Dr. Spot was just Spot, a lazy oaf with a huge appetite and no sense of purpose. Now he's so busy, he hardly has time to eat. Thank you for giving him a new leash on life.

Y. Miranner,
Seattle, Washington

And here's what some well-known personalities have to say about the power dogs have to heal:

"I want to acknowledge dogs fully for the space they create in my life to experience an opportunity to expand my aliveness."

Werner Airheart

"They say let sleeping dogs lie, but hey, no sleeping dog's ever lied to me."

Yogi Bearer

"Nature has designed the dog to be dymaxion—they give a maximum output of love from a minimum input of food."

Duckminster Fuller

". . . and they called it Puppy Love."

Paul Anka

So open your heart up to the paws that refreshes. And remember, dogs are nonhabit-forming and have no unpleasant side effects (provided you watch where you're stepping).

Because animals are such sweet, trusting, and gentle souls, the question arises, should we eat animals? As you may know, there is a great guru down in Texas who actually advocates eating beef. His name is Baba Q. You see, it is generally considered bad karma to eat meat because most meat does not want to be eaten. But if it did want to be eaten, it would then be good karma to eat it. That's where Baba Q comes in. He has a special retreat for cows down in Texas— he calls it a hashram—where he teaches them to want to be eaten. First, he puts them into a deep trance state, which he calls cattlepsy. Then he brings in top-notch motivational speakers to get them to totally embrace cattlehood so they can move up on the food chain next time they incarnate. By the time the last day of the training arrives, these cattle are so full of enthusiasm, they are on their hind legs chanting, "Hold the pickle, hold the lettuce, butchers' cleavers won't upset us."

After the training, they settle into a state of serenity which can only be described as peaceful cow-existence, as they calmly await their fate. And what you have is 100 percent grounded beef. Incidentally, Baba Q runs a very strict hashram. When they come of calf-bearing age, all of his cows and bulls must get married. That way, they always have a legitimate beef. The bulls find they have more stability in life having a significant udder. And when the cows come home, they always have someone to come home to.

One thing I learned when I studied with Broken Wind was how much the Native American tradition respects all animals. When they are about to eat an animal, they humbly ask its permission to eat it. Now, the average American never thinks to do this, and this can have grave consequences. As an example, Colonel Sanders was haunted in his later years by ghosts of the many chickens he fried. Yes, it is not uncommon for chickens to come home to roost this way, in the form of poultrygeists.

Fortunately, there is a greater consciousness nowadays about the sanctity of animal life. A new movie bears this out. It is about a young deer who is so disturbed by his cousins in the woods being shot by hunters, that he decides to get revenge. The movie is called "Bambo."

THE PLANT KINGDOM

Everyone is so concerned with the greenhouse effect nowadays. Personally, I'm more concerned with the outhouse effect due to our effluent society. Taking a good toxic dump in the woods or in some stream may feel good to us, but it's choking the life out of the flora and fauna. It is particularly difficult for our friends the trees when we mess up their neighborhood. It's not like they can move. When trees put down roots, it is for life. So if we want our flora to go on floricating and our fauna to—uh, be fruitful and multiply, we must be conscious of the chemical wastes we are leaving behind.

You know what the most serious social problem on the planet is? I will tell you. It is chemical dependency. And these chemicals we are dependent on can cause dangerous hallucinations—one being that we need them to grow our food, build our homes, and medicate our bodies. Petrochemical pushers have gotten the soil so addicted to herbicides and pesticides that it cannot produce without them. So I say, *Just Say No to Chemical Dependency!*

Sure, we should get our young people to stop abusing

substances, but what about the substances abusing them? If you think killer weed leaves harmful residues in the body, wait until you see what weed killer does. Broken Wind, the great Native American shaman, had a definition for weed killer—a chemical substance that kills living things, some of which are weeds.

Forget the argument that "everyone is doing it" or "just a little bit is harmless." Studies show that farmers who start out using herbicide are more likely to move on to the harder stuff—like food irradiation. We must kick our chemical habit now and go organic. Let's check the planet into a good detox program and get our soil high on life, otherwise there will be no life to get high on.

You see, I've been conversing with plants and trees for years (I made it my business to learn the moss code), and I can tell you that trees think we humans are becoming a pain in the grass, although to be perfectly fair we do make decent food after we've been in the ground for a while. (Even though humans take credit for inventing just about everything, it is a scientific fact that trees have had food processors for millions of years. They are called worms.) And yet, as exasperated as they are with us, trees are willing to go out on a limb and open their branches to their biped cousins.

Plants have much to teach us, not only when it comes to aligning with nature, but also about fulfilling ourselves. They are sad when they see that too few of us humans ever flower, and far too many go to seed. Their message is simple: Whatever manure you've been through, consider it fertilizer because we are all meant to blossom.

Yes, it is a jungle out there. And it's a good thing. Because trees and plants are our planet's lungs. So I suggest we turn over a new leaf. Let's begin restoring the rain forest as the first step in a Planetary Aerobics Program to make sure our

Mother Earth stays fit for life. All of this money spent trying to reach out to other planets—how about reaching out to our own? Let's not worry about the little green guys from outer space and focus instead on the little green guys in our own backyard—because they are rooting for us. Let's never forget the valuable gift God gave us on the Third Day when He said, "This Bud's for you."

THE MINERAL KINGDOM

We have come to appreciate animal intelligence, and even plant consciousness. So now it is time to converse with our friends in the mineral kingdom. Although rocks come on like the strong silent type, they actually possess a great intelligence. We forget they're beings, too, and we take them for granite. But at this point in our development, these rocks and crystals are necessary to help us resonate with the earth. For are they not chips off the old block? We are about to enter a new stone age, and I for one am very excited about it.

It is true. I am one of the biggest rock fans. There is a great spiritual master on the planet today who is known as the "Rock Guru." His name is Baba Oom Mow Mow, and his message is simple: "Listen to the Stones," he says, "and the Crystals and the Diamonds, and Ruby and the Romantics, and especially Garnet Mimms and the Enchanters, for they will teach you about balanced harmonies." And we very much need to balance our harmonies, my children. Crystals will be able to restore this balance, because they are great conductors.

Many people have asked me what I think about healing stones and I say, "It's about time!" We have abused them long enough, so why not heal them? We've stepped on them, crushed them, mined them, thrown them. So let's try healing them. Obviously, acupuncture will not work, but how about a massage? Polishing can be very healing.

You may think the average rock is hard and unfeeling, but beneath that rough, tough exterior is a very sensitive being. I walk past yards and dumps and I cannot help but notice how many pet rocks have been abandoned. Sure, we petted them for a while, cuddled them, maybe even slept with them. But then we saw they didn't do any clever tricks. We got bored, so we just tossed them away. I mean, do we have hearts of stone?

The people of Atlantis mistreated their friends from the mineral kingdom and you know what happened to them. Ages ago, Atlanteans used crystals to power aircraft and heat homes. But they lost everything because they abused their crystals! How did they abuse them? Well, aside from spanking and yelling at them, they made the crystals perform unnatural acts—like manipulating and brainwashing people.

During the "coming good years," polluting energy sources will be replaced with New Clear Energy. And there will be abundant energy for everyone! All of us will have our own energy fields which we will harvest as needed. Crystals will help attune us so we can receive energy from the Universal Transmitter. Now, we're used to network broadcasting with lots of commercials and mindless violence. Believe me, with the crystal sets we all will have, we'll be getting channels we can't even imagine now. Our pictures will be less fuzzy, the colors will be brighter, and more of us will ourselves become Tell-A-Vision transmitters.

Precious gems can also be very healing, but the biggest problem with them seems to be all the mining going on. People see a precious stone, and they say, "Mine!" and then someone else goes, "Mine!" and before long, you have a war going on. In recent centuries, precious stones have mostly been associated with the upper crust, but often the most valuable things are found below the surface. So now maybe we need to do a different kind of mining—uncovering the gem that is in each of us.

Some Gemstones and Their Properties

Abalone. This gemstone provides protection from impure or negative thoughts. When you wear this stone on your person and you encounter falsehood, it seems to broadcast a message to your brain that says, "Abalone, abalone, ah-baloney!"

Agate. Can be very helpful in identifying an ailment, great for uncovering problems. Problems get very embarrassed when they are naked, and they slink off and don't bother you any more. Also good for acceptance. Agate reminds us, "This too shall pass," which makes it excellent for people with kidney stones.

Amethyst. Increases spiritual awareness. Inexplicably, when people first use this stone they have an uncontrollable urge to go out and buy Mahalia Jackson records.

Aquamarine. This stone helps create a feeling of peace in the heart. Better to open the heart this way than have a surgeon do it.

Chrysolite. This is the gemstone for clear sight. It helps you focus your vision. Great for the gaze. (But straight people can benefit from it, too.)

Diamond. The king of all gemstones. Diamonds are a girl's best friend, and when you consider that man's best friend is a dog, it should be crystal clear why women are far harder to shop for.

Emerald. Helps you see different levels. In the highrise of consciousness, too many of us are stuck on the mezzanine—and are looking down. Helps elevate vibrations and keeps you from getting stuck between floors.

Garnet. This precious stone helps you get to the truth. Many Americans suffer from truth decay, particularly if their television diet consists of sugary situation comedies or crime shows containing high levels of assault. If you can't use mental floss after each viewing, try garnets.

Jasper. Helps you become more well-rounded. Perfect for squares.

Lapis Lazuli. Enhances openness. Swami reports: "I wore it one day, and people smiled at me wherever I went. I attributed it to my openness, and sure enough after several hours I noticed—my fly was open."

Quartz. Makes your transmission more fluid while you're moving into surpassing gear. If you can handle working with quartz at the beginning, that is fine. If not, you can work yourself up by starting with pintz.

Samsonite. Great for people who are carrying a lot of spiritual baggage onto the higher planes. Because it is light, you'll have an easier time making the weight requirements.

Topaz. A beautiful stone made from the fossilized, hardened "paz" that collects between the toes, it reminds us of the earthly beauty of all things—including the stuff that collects between the toes.

THE REALM OF THE MAN-MADE

Let's face it, life is frought with responsibilities. Not only do we have to brush our teeth after every meal, balance our checkbooks, water the plants, and change the kitty litter, but we have to take care of whatever we create—otherwise it results in unsightly "karmic build-up" which can ruin future lifetimes. Yes, over the past few centuries in particular we have taken on the role of Creator as we have manufactured all sorts of entities not only to help us with our work, but to play with us and be our companions as well. Even though it is considered a bit tacky to turn down social engagements by saying, "No, thanks. I promised my television I would stay home and watch it," a lot of people really do think of their bicycle or computer or TV as their best friend.

When I am around these machine spirits, I must tell you, I feel very keenly how they look to us as Creators. I was once around a group of Buicks that were being recalled because of manufacturer error, and I picked up this tremendous sense of betrayal. In fact, these cars were having a theological discussion and one made a valid point: "If we were the product of a Loving Creator, why would we be sent to Meet our Maker with so few miles on our odometer?" (I think that is why our Creator gave us humans free will. He just took a look at our maintenance schedule, multiplied that by several billion, and said, "If I don't make these entities self-correcting, they'll always be in the shop—and I can just forget about ever playing golf.")

Most of my experience with machine entities comes from the karma yoga work I did while studying with Harry Cohen Baba. When he suggested I get a job with a social service organization, I noticed that I felt a particular affinity for the abandoned cars I saw along the streets in New York. So I got a job as a counselor at a truck abuse clinic in the Bronx, and the things I saw made me double-clutch. Neglected vehicles that had been left out to rust in the cold winter, vehicles with their windshields smashed by neighborhood toughs who

hated foreign cars, cars that needed vast amounts of recon-
structive surgery but couldn't get fixed because they didn't
have insurance. The saddest thing was the older cars who
looked forward to being retired. Often the owner would look
to see what new tires would cost and say, "I'm sorry, but I just
don't have your retirement money." And the poor old heap
would get shipped to the junk yard to be carved up for
transplants and cremated.

Then there was the outreach work I did with thousands of
unemployed vehicles that sat languishing on the lot. These
poor entities could not understand why they had been sold
or traded. "Yah sure, I been grinding and squeaking last
coupla years," said one aging Swedish car. "But cars like me,
we built tough! Look at that engine compression—better
than a car half my age. But in this old rusted body, who
would know? I look around here, I get depressed. I say to
myself, is this gonna be my final lot in life?" Saab stories like
this were not uncommon. Some of these cars felt bitter, some
felt resigned. All felt used.

So I comforted and counseled these poor vehicles. Sometimes I would just loosen their radiator caps and let them
blow off some steam. Other times I did past life readings with
them. Of course, autos are reincarnated. And many of these
vehicles perked up as they remembered adventures as early
pioneers on the first dirt roads or as actors in Hollywood
movies, or as playthings of the rich and famous. Of course,
karma (not to mention truckma) came into play as well. One
vehicle, which had been a getaway car used by Bonnie and
Clyde, had to suffer through a miserable lifetime as a sickly
Fiat that was always in the shop. I think this past life work
helped restore a lot of pride, as many old and unattractive
vehicles began to sport "I was a Mercedes in a previous
lifetime" bumper stickers.

After several months at the truck abuse clinic, I realized that more than anything else, these poor vehicles needed spiritual healing. Many had lost their drive. They would idle their day away, or sit motionless waiting for someone, anyone, to open them up and turn them on. There were a few miracles, probably due to the radiator water we were using from Lourdes. But something else was needed. One day, in a desperate attempt to jump-start a beat-up old Plymouth whose battery had given out, I began to softly whisper affirmations in its vent window: "Every cell in your battery is fully charged and you can feel it to the bottom of your soulanoid." "You are an enthusiastic self-starter who literally jumps out of the garage each morning."

Miraculously, the Plymouth made a full recovery and within two weeks had attracted a new owner who restored it to mint condition. Today the Plymouth is a regular at classic car shows and often appears in movies and commercials. And that is when I realized that I could heal cars spiritually—and mechanically—through the power of suggestion. So now, to help you heal your automobile without harmful engine additives or invasive mechanical work, here is my Auto-Suggestion Meditation. Just repeat this to your car once a day, and within a month's time your car will miraculously shed miles from its odometer reading.

SWAMI BEYONDANANDA'S AUTO-SUGGESTION MEDITATION

Turn off your ignition and put yourself into park. Let your weight sink slowly into your tires. Let your shock absorbers release all the tensions of the road. Ah, you are dieseling. Your diet is too rich, and your gas line is clogged. Now take a gentle breath and send it to your gas line. Good. Your gas line is now a clear channel and you are able to pass your gas with ease. You say you are troubled by bad brakes? Look at your bad brakes as opportunities. Have faith in the Master Cylinder, and you will have better brakes the next time around. Your catalytic converter is divinely inspired. It is telling all those impure particles that if they do not convert, then they will surely burn! Your exhaust system expells all toxic fumes as a fine, perfumed, pink powder. (I know your four-wheel drive power wagon is going to have a problem with this one, but tell me, what is more important—the environment, or your muscle car's macho ego?) Your front wheels are aligned with perfection. YOU ARE NOW AT ONE WITH YOUR UNIVERSAL JOINT.

Swami Answers all Your Questions About Tell-A-Vision and the Major Channels.

Dear Swami:
Are you a strict vegetarian? What do you think of tofu?
                                    Gorman Dize,
                                    San Antonio, Texas

Dear Gorman:
    Actually, I rarely think of tofu. At a gathering recently someone offered me some and I politely declined. And the person said, "But it is the food of the future, Swami." And I said, "That is good. Let's keep it that way." Actually, I am not a vegetarian. I am a humanitarian. I eat people. And I will tell you why. You've heard the saying, "You are what you eat?" Well, it is true. We take on the energy of any entity we ingest. That is why I recommend that we eat only the most realized beings on the planet. I have started a new program called, "Swallow The Leader," and donor cards are available. I

mean, if you can donate your body to a medical school, why not donate it to a cooking school? You know what we Humanitarians say—the best way to serve humankind is by *being* served.

★

Dear Swami:

I've heard it is possible to reincarnate in some of the lower forms, such as animals, insects, even plants. My psychic told me that we humans can even reincarnate as pigeons. Please tell me this is not so!

Mick Stupp,
Millheim, Pennsylvania

Dear Mick:

It may surprise you to know that humans can be reincarnated in all of these lower forms—even plants. It is all based on the laws of karma. For example, there is the case of the man who was a terrible polluter in his lifetime. He was reincarnated as a sewage treatment plant. As for your concern about pigeons, I've got some bad news and some good news. The bad news is, yes, you can come back as a pigeon. The good news is, you'll finally be able to make a deposit on that BMW.

★

Dear Swami:

I have heard that you communicate with beings from outer space all the time. Why are they visiting us? What are they trying to accomplish, anyway?

Howie Yaduin,
Paramus, New Jersey

Dear Howie:

I know there has been much speculation about this, but now the real reason for these visits can be told. You know that in spirit we are all one, but in form—the differences are unbelievable. You see, most of the beings in other parts of the universe have the ability to change form at will. And you will be happy to note that our planet is known throughout the universe as a pioneer in design. So many of the so-called U.F.O. sightings we have had in the past are merely other beings coming to check out the latest "fashions." For example, on one planet all the beings look and speak like Donald Duck. On another, everyone looks like a '57 Chevy. You would be amazed if you could see the *real* Miss Universe contest.

Of course, this changing of forms can have tragic consequences as well. Like the one planet that decided the ultimate form was the Pillsbury Dough Boy. On the first hot day, they all went to the beach and by the end of the day—well, they had a group transcendent experience. They all rose to meet their baker.

★

Dear Swami:
If everything on Earth has a purpose, why are there roaches?

Barry Yareef,
Glendale, California

Dear Barry:
Indeed, roaches are great teachers for us all. They are among the most persistent life forms on the planet and can thrive in the most adverse conditions. Most importantly, they are living proof that you don't have to be beautiful or well-liked to be successful.

★

Dear Swami:
Is it true that dolphins are more intelligent than humans? Also, what are you doing to save the whales?

Hugh Millity,
New Haven, Connecticut

Dear Hugh:

Oh, yes. They are much more intelligent than people, and the reasons are quite apparent. Think about it. As far as I know, the dolphins don't capture us humans, put us in an artificial environment called "Land World," and teach us to do stupid pet tricks like catching hamburgers in our mouths. This by itself makes them more intelligent. Meanwhile, we're dumping medical debris and toxic waste into their living room. And still they tolerate us, love us even. They rarely complain, although lately they are starting to beach a little bit. That is why I am working very hard to save the whales. In fact, I have been working with what is called the "Underwater Bible Project." That is where thousands of Bibles are dumped into the ocean each year in hopes that the whales will read them—and be saved. To raise money for this worthy cause I am selling Save the Whale bumper stickers which read: "He ain't heavy, he's my blubber."

★

Dear Swami:

How do you feel about wild game preserves?

Moe Slikely,
Bisbee, Arizona

Dear Moe:

I've never tried them, but it sounds pretty disgusting. I would just stick with the usual strawberry and apricot.

☆ PART FOUR
Towards
Nonjudgment Day

SURE THERE ARE ALREADY MORE THAN ENOUGH religions out there. But not one of them has figured out how to keep all of these "faiths" from fighting about who God loves most. That is why I am introducing a new religion, FUNdamentalism—where the fun comes before the mental. And if people follow this path, they'll have so much fun they'll forget to hate and forget to judge. Indeed, the purpose of this religion is to bring about Nonjudgment Day, when all the peoples of the world will lay down their arms. We will look kind of foolish with our arms on the ground and our butts sticking up in the air, but peace will reign—because it is impossible to attack anyone while in this position (unless you have just eaten burritos).

Yes, the world situation is serious if not grave. But as FUNdamentalism teaches, the best way to overcome gravity is with levity. The advent of Nonjudgment Day is inevitable.

How do we know? It has already been predicted in those ancient Egyptian scrolls, the Tut Sea Rolls, which maintain that Nonjudgment Day is near when the nations of the world begin each session of the United Nations with the Hokey Pokey. Now picture that for a moment. We've all seen those bumper stickers that say, "Visualize World Peace." That is much too abstract. Visualize the U.N. doing the Hokey Pokey, then tell everyone you know to do the same. Through the principle of Tell-A-Vision, it will come about. And that is just the beginning. Once the nations of the world have mastered the Hokey Pokey, then they can move on to the more advanced dances—like the Bunny Hop. That is a very powerful healing dance because, for once, everyone will be connected and moving in the same direction. People say, "Swami, why are you trying to change the world?" And I answer that I am *not* trying to change the world. We've tried that and it doesn't work. I say let's *toilet train* the world and we will never have to change it again!

LESSON 10: BRINGING ABOUT WORLD PEACE BY CREATING A STATE OF WAR

Yep. There are some good years coming. But if we destroy the planet, we're certainly going to miss them. While being dead has some advantages—getting up in the morning is no longer a problem and you're never bothered with jury duty—dead people, blonde or brunette, definitely have less fun. No, if we are going to have good years, we need people—and if we want to have people we can't have war, particularly nuclear war. That is why I have come up with a unique plan that will guarantee peace by creating a state of war.

You know, weapons are a lot like cigarettes. Even though all the studies show they're bad for your health, people buy them anyway. You know how people say they want to quit and the next day they're bumming a cigarette off of you? Well, war is like that, too. Everyone says they want to quit fighting, but in the next breath they say to us, "Gimme a six-pack of M-16s and a carton of ammo—to go." I tell you it is a deadly habit, even for those who don't indulge.

Not that I have anything against soldiering, which is the second oldest profession. But it was different in the old days, when warriors were only permitted to smite other warriors. You'd go to a village all juiced up for a good battle and someone would say, "I'm sorry, this is the Non-smoting section. If you want Smoting, you'll have to go over there." That is why I think the easiest way to bring about world peace is to create a State of War, and I think that state should be Nevada.

Under my plan, all those who want to fight wars will be able to do so in a confined space, and the rest of us can play volleyball or eat pistachio ice cream or watch our kids grow up. Just think. Every summer, all the warlike tribes can gather and pommel each other senseless to their heart's content. It can be called the "Rambo Gathering." One more suggestion. While I would not ban weapons—after all, war between consenting adults should be permitted in a free society—I *would* ban ammunition.

Of course, not everybody is thrilled with my plan. Rev. U.R. "Tim" Tayshin, who represents the Mortal Majority, thinks the plan will encourage immortality among our youth. "When people stop dying for their country," he says, "our entire mortal fiber is doomed. First it's their country they're not dying for, then it's their religion. Before too long, people aren't dying at all. I tell you, it isn't fair!"

More important than creating this State of War is what we do to create peace within ourselves. The first step to bring peace into your heart (without having to have a peacemaker surgically installed) is to cut down on assault. Sure, it's natural to get angry from time to time, but you must realize that the words you choose to express your anger are of utmost importance. No matter what you are feeling, you must always have words of peace on your lips. Therefore, I suggest the following: The next time you want to explode about a situation, shout, "Ah, peace on it!"

The good news is, peace on earth is inevitable. I sure hope we human beings are around to enjoy it. We must become nomads—that is when you no mad at me, I no mad at you. When we are all nomads, there will truly be nomadness on the planet. And it all begins with each individual. This may seem like a peacemeal approach to transforming the world, but it works. A little peace here, a little peace there, and pretty soon all the peaces will fit together to make one big peace everywhere.

LESSON 11: FISCAL FITNESS FOR EVERYONE

You know, we are living in a competitive world, and this has been so for a very long time, especially in the so-called civilized world. It is said that one of the first signs of civilization was people decorating their bodies. They would put on jewelry, various forms of makeup, clothing, armor, ceremonial garb—and the more people had on, the better they would feel about themselves. In fact, many anthropologists believe this was the origin of the word "moron."

Now we can look at a great person like Gandhi—who was one of the most significant beings of our century even though he had less on than most people—and we can see his less-on was more valuable to us than the material wealth of all the more-ons in history. The truth is, no matter what we wear on the outside, our inner being shines forth who we really are. Now before you go looking for an interior decorator to find hangings for your intestinal wall, relax a minute! Forget about redecorating, about changing yourself. You are a unique, one-of-a-kind masterpiece. When you were made, the Creator threw away the mold. And it is a good thing because a lot of people are allergic to mold.

In the FUNdamentalist religion, we don't celebrate Christmas per se. To us, every day is Christmas, because every day is the day to give our gifts freely. In fact, we are the gift. So if you're looking for a stocking stuffer, look no further than your own feet. Because you, my children, must step forward to share your gift. Now a lot of people say, "I would love to share my gift and do what I love to do, but I just don't seem to have the financial energy to get over the hump." Well, that is a common problem, children. And that is why you must learn the principles and practices of Fiscal Fitness. And while in our hearts we want to make sure no one goes hungry (unless they are dieting, because they have experienced too much abundance), it is more practical to teach Fiscal Fitness to the masses than to try to take care of them ourselves. It's common sense—you can fuel some of the people some of the time, but you can't fuel all of the people all of the time.

How Swami Beyondananda Mastered the Fiscal Plane

I have not always had what you people would call a prosperity consciousness. I tasted poverty at a very early age. And it tasted very much like Spam. You laugh at Spam, but while you are laughing, there are people who are making millions of dollars selling Spam through a multi-level marketing system. The company is called Spamway, and they are promoting Spam as the ultimate survival food—because it is guaranteed to be the last thing on your shelf.

Anyway, I was not prepared for prosperity during my early years. For example, I hold my high school football coach responsible for my early financial difficulties, because he told me repeatedly that I had an inability to receive. As a result, some years later I found myself in New York City going through what I call my "Baroque Period." I was so Baroque, I was Haydn from the landlord. Anyway, one month I received a notice that said if I did not pay my electric bill, they would shut off my power. Now at that time, I had just begun working with the power of thought, so I began affirming that a large check would arrive that very day. Minutes later, the doorbell rang. It was a huge Czechoslovakian guy who said he had come to shut off my electricity. It was then that I learned an important lesson—the Universe cannot spell.

But I knew I was on the right track. I began to read everything I could about prosperity. One day my guru, Harry Cohen Baba, handed me a copy of *Reader's Digest*, and there I found the article that would change my life: "I Upped My Income, Up Yours," by a man named Midas Welby-Rich. One affirmation in particular jumped out at me:

"I am literally bowled over by prosperity." For three days, I repeated this mantra every waking minute. On the fourth day, it happened. I was crossing Lexington Avenue near 37th Street, and I was so absorbed in my mantra that I didn't see it coming. Suddenly, from out of nowhere, this Brinks truck turned the corner and knocked me silly.

And that, children, changed my life.

I was able to live quite comfortably on the settlement money for several years, and this enabled me to support my personal growth habit, not to mention two lawyers and a chiropractor.

I have subsequently learned a far less painful way to bring money into my life, which I will share with you absolutely free. (Actually, I am not as altruistic as you might think. I've run up quite a karmic debt over the centuries and I figure this might handle at least some of the interest payments.)

Do you want to turn money from a medium of exchange into an extra large? Would you like to turn cash flow constipation into generous runs of prosperity? Then listen very carefully and repeat this mantra before every meal:

"Everything I eat turns to money—and my drawers are full of cash."

May prosperity move through you always.

Are You Fiscally Fit? Take This Simple Quiz

1. Does most of your fiscal exercise come from bouncing checks and running up large tabs?

2. Do you wait until the last minute each year to pay your taxes and then go numb and clammy when you see how much you have to hand over to the IRS (taxic shock syndrome)?

3. When a store clerk tells you, "We take credit cards," do you say, "That's okay, mine have already been taken"?

4. Is your idea of an affordable vacation watching "Life-styles of the Rich and Famous" on TV?

5. Has your savings account been cancelled due to lack of interest?

6. Did you give your last $5,000 to your broker to invest, and now *you're* broker?

7. Are you so overwhelmed by bills that you're beginning to hear invoices in the night?

8. Did you turn your mutual funds into parimutuel funds—and your horse failed to finish?

9. Did you follow your banker's advice and put all your money into CD's, and now you have no money left to buy a CD player?

10. When you were told to convert your holdings to liquid assets, did you go out and buy beer?

0–2 "Yes" answers: You're in great fiscal condition. In fact, your ticker is in much better shape than Wall Street's.

3–5 "Yes" answers: You're in pretty good shape, but your buy-ceps are a bit overdeveloped.

6–8 "Yes" answers: You'd be in better shape if you exercised your restraint more. I'd suggest finding a shop-arone to accompany you to stores to make sure you don't spend too much.

More than 8 "Yes" answers. You're a fiscal wreck.

THE PRINCIPLES OF FISCAL FITNESS

Principle Number One: No Matter How Spiritual You Are, You Have to Learn to Live on the Fiscal Plane

The truth is, there is no way for those of us in bodies to separate the fiscal from the spiritual. Sure, the best things in life are free—the sun, the sky, clouds, rocks. But food, that will cost you extra. As will a place to stay, for that matter. And something to drive around in. As my guru, Harry Cohen Baba, was fond of saying, "The lilies of the valley toileth not—nor do they drive BMW's."

Principle Number Two: Make Sure You are Doing the Right Fiscal Exercises

I hate to say this, but our economy is really out of shape. And the exercises we're doing to try to get *into* shape—like stretching a line of credit—are making it worse. You see, we all do it. We see something we like and say, "This seems like a good buy," and we buy it. Then we see another good buy, and we buy that. It's a good buy here, and a good buy there, and pretty soon it's goodbye money. Meanwhile, the merchants are doing push-ups. They are pushing up their prices because they know we're gonna buy anyway. But anyone who's studied buyology knows the buying has to stop when we run out of money. And I'm afraid we're now on the brink of fiscal exhaustion.

Fortunately, there is a solution. I suggest we give our spending muscles a break and exercise our self-control instead. You might experiment with the sell-a-bit lifestyle. Instead of buying, buying, buying you should try to sell a bit of what you own. We can also improve our circulation by giving away what we can't sell.

Principle Number Three: If You're Going to Play the Stock Market, Commitment is the Key

People often ask me if I think the stock market is going to crash. Well, I am strictly nonprophet, so I don't usually make predictions. But I will say this. When I visited the New York Stock Exchange this summer, they were installing seat belts. Now of course, there will still be those of you who insist on playing the stock market. So I will give you some valuable information. According to Yuan Tibet, the great Dowist finance-seer, the secret to success in the stock market is, in a word, commitment. "Anyone who puts his hard-earned money into the stock market," he says, "should definitely be committed."

Now I will offer one very specific tip that he passed along to me. You know the 3M Company, the one that makes Scotch Tape? They're about to merge with the company that makes M & M's and become the 5M Company. They'll be making a new kind of candy called M & M & M & M & M's, and it's guaranteed to stick to your mouth, your hands, and even the walls. So, investors, take heart. There is still plenty of bull left on Wall Street.

Principle Number Four: Raise the Interest Rate

Yes, I know that most financial experts believe that raising the interest rates at this time would lead to depression, but I think just the opposite would happen. With all the interesting things to do on this planet, it should be at least 80 or 90 percent! You see, if people began doing more of the things they were interested in, there'd be no depression. They'd be too busy having fun to feel anxious about money. So I say, stop sitting on your assets, my children. Invest in whatever interests you.

Principle Number Five: Don't Get So Caught Up in the Fiscal that You Neglect the Metafiscal

There is this ridiculous rumor going around lately that the international bankers are plotting to buy up the entire world. I mean, wake up! Who do you think owns the world? The truth is, they're trying like crazy to sell the world, and they're in a big hurry. They want to unload it before the cleaning bill comes.

And who would they sell it to? Two main groups—the Extra-terrestials and the Channeled Entities. What the government hasn't told us about those ETs is that they generally are reported to be wearing gold coats. In other words, they are intergalactic real estate agents! As for the disembodied entities, they are trying to drive the real estate prices down with all their doomsday talk. That way, all the humans on earth will move to Oregon and Washington. Think about it. You don't hear them telling folks to move to Hawaii or Palm Beach, do you?

You know, I get a lot of these doomsday prophecies. People ask me all the time, "What is the best investment for the coming years? Should we be buying futures?" And my advice is, don't worry. Be here now! Forget about buying futures. Buy presents instead. You know how some of the self-sovereignty people suggest we invest in diamonds and hoard food? I say, invest in hearts—and give food away.

LESSON 12: THE COMIC-KAZE PATH

So, assuming that the Tut Sea Rolls are most probably correct and Nonjudgment Day is near, what can the average guy do? Well, he can wait passively for Nonjudgment to come from heaven. Or he can get out there, spread the fun and who knows—maybe help bring it about faster. For those who feel they are on a mission from God to raise our planet's laugh expectancy, I offer a unique challenge: Become a Comic-kaze. A Comic-kaze is someone who uses lightness to illuminate darkness, levity to overcome gravity. Someone who enjoys laughmaking as much as lovemaking. You know how boy scouts help people across the street? Comic-kazes do the same kinds of good deeds, only they help people to the sunny side of the street. And they are full of surprises, too. They are the kind of people who go to shopping malls and, when no one is looking, pour bubble bath into the fountains to remind people that the only kind of pain worth having is champagne.

How Swami Became a FUNdamentalist

As you already know by now, I was blessed at an early age with the gift of levity. No matter how serious the situation, I always managed to be in the light place at the light time. In high school, I spent much of my spare time in my room blissfully floating around the ceiling. One day, my mother walked in and said, "It's time for you to stop hanging around the house and get a job."

So I got an after-school job as a cowboy, and I really enjoyed getting to know the cows. This may surprise you, but cattle have a terrific sense of humor. Their dry delivery, their straight-faced double takes, their impeccable sense of timing. Sure, much of their humor is of the slapstick variety—stepping in the bucket just as you've finished milking or dropping a chocolate pie on your new Frye boots —but their facial expressions are worthy of Jack Benny. Believe me, no one can milk an audience better than a cow.

I enjoyed an idyllic few weeks working with the cows and encouraging their humorous self-expression. They tend to be shy performers as far as animals go (pigs, on the other hand, are natural hams), but before long they felt sufficiently relaxed to show up for milking wearing outlandish hats and clown noses. Just when I felt the most positive about the work I was doing, I was unexpectedly fired by the farmer, who accused me of turning his cattle into a laughingstock.

Deciding that a change of scenery was in order, I left for New York City where I met my greatest teacher of all, Harry Cohen Baba. It was the fabled Garment Center Saint who initiated me into the path of the Comic-kaze, the ancient Oriental art of Fu Ling. What marvels I found in those teachings! After just a month I had increased my jest measurements by 50 percent, and had mastered some very intricate mime control techniques. My old levity had returned, so much so that when meditating outdoors I had to tie myself to a post to keep from floating away.

Fu Ling became my life. I quickly learned the forms of Jo King and Tai Ming, which allowed me to throw quick punchlines repeatedly without tiring. "Remember," Harry Cohen Baba used to say, "muscles make you muscle-bound, but a sense of humor can move mountains. There is no defense against a well-delivered punchline." I learned how to lob one-liners; an explosion of laughter from the audience told me I had hit the target. "If you want to rise in this business," my beloved master would say, "you have to know how to fall." So I practiced pratfalls until I had a full-blown case of psorasses. Unable to sit down, I concentrated on stand-up. I became adept at coffee-spitting, the ancient comedic technique of expressing surprise.

But then a funny thing happened (actually, when you are a Comic-kaze-in-training, everything that happens is funny, so I am speaking figuratively here). I would be in the midst of laughing uproariously and I would stop, just like that, and say to myself, "There's nothing funny about this at all." And then the next time, the same thing would happen. Right in the middle of laughing, I would stop. Well, this disturbed me greatly. Something was playing havoc with my laugh force.

When I relayed my symptoms to Harry Cohen Baba, he said, "Ah, yes. You are going through your mid-laugh crisis. There is no more I can teach you. It is time for you to make one last trek before you hit the Big Show. You must venture into the subways and ply your trade there, for there will soon be a big market for underground comics. Do this, and one day you will be fooly realized."

Thus began what I call my "missing years," when no one—not even I—knew what I was doing. Like many young seekers, I was trying to find myself. I know now that I was looking in all the wrong places—the Metropolitan Opera House, the ladies' lingerie department at Macy's, Madison Square Garden on pro wrestling night—places I wouldn't ever dream of going. This one day, I was meditating at a subway station in Brooklyn, curled up in my Full Lettuce Pose (I was working on developing my food consciousness in those days). I began to feel a funny sensation at the top of my head. At first, I thought it was a rabbit nibbling away at me, but when I opened my eyes I saw it was a kid about twelve years old who was very concertedly drilling his knuckles into my skull. Since there are no accidents (except occasionally on the Encinada Freeway just north of the Slauson cut-off), I realized that this had to be the healing I had asked for. This was confirmed when I saw "Canarsie Angels" emblazoned on the back of his black leather jacket. "Say, what do you fellas call this?" I asked.

"Noogies," was the reply. (I later found out that the actual scientific term for this treatment is "Brooklyn Acupressure.")

As I relaxed into the hands of this gifted young healer, I could feel my kundalini stirring all up through my spine. This was good because all the cosmic cookbooks tell you that if you don't continuously stir your kundalini, it ends up in a congealed blob down in your lower chakras. And then I felt a volcanic rush of energy coursing through the top of my head, and it seemed to explode in a flash of color. At this point, I opened my eyes and was shocked to see that my hair was standing straight out and was now rainbow colored! And in this great moment of revelation, emblazoned in my mind, were, the Five Keys to Eternal Laugh.

I took the train back downtown to the ashram of my guru, Harry Cohen Baba. I would have felt greatly embarrassed about my hair, except this was New York City and nobody seemed to notice. Harry Cohen Baba took one look at me and said, "Looks like you've been struck by enlightening. Mazel tov!"

"But Garment Centered One," I asked, "why did my hair turn all these colors?"

"Don't be silly," he said. "That always happens when you open your clown chakra."

THE FIVE KEYS TO ETERNAL LAUGH

Key Number One:

"And on the Eighth Day, God saw the world was funny, and She created Laughter."

Life is a situation comedy that will never get cancelled, and if you listen carefully you will find that a laugh track has been provided. Our purpose is to be At Fun with the Universe. This is called Atfunment. Whenever we feel the least bit out of balance—guilty, sad, fearful, envious—we must reaffirm our FUNness. We can do this by slapping the knee and repeating the mantra "Ha" in rapid succession until you fall down in ecstatic rapture (take it easy at first so as not to rapture your jocular vein).

Key Number Two:

"Thou shalt not practice mirth control."

Of course, unplanned mirths can sometimes cause problems—like in the middle of a funeral—but every mirth is an expression of the Laugh Force, and it must not be interfered with. Even though there is still some question as to when a laugh begins, it is always inappropriate to abort a laugh. If you don't want this mirth for yourself, go through with it anyway—and give it away to someone who needs it. It is never right to snuff out another's laugh or interfere in any way with the natural laugh cycle.

Key Number Three:

"When you find a sacred cow, milk it for all it is worth."

Sacred cows, like everything else in Creation, were put here to be laughed at. Since the Universe is not sexist, the same holds true for sacred bull—or what we term "taboos." A taboo comes from putting a band-aid, or tab, over a boo-boo. It is a rule of life that all boo-boos heal, provided they get fresh air and light. When we cover a boo-boo and turn it into a taboo, we keep out the light. Laughter is a gentle way to pull off the band-aid, and when the sore spot is illumined by the Laugh Force, it heals once and for all.

Key Number Four:

"Laugh at adversity, though you be tittering on the brink of disaster."

The cardinal rule of Laugh Eternal is, laugh, laugh, laugh heartily and uproariously—even if you don't see what's so funny. You may not get the joke right away—just follow the laugh track. You'll get it eventually. We all do. We are cosmic comics who have come to the material world for one reason only—to get more material. Laugh at yourself, and the whole world will laugh at you, too.

Key Number Five:

"Eternal Laugh is here and now."

We need not wait for the Man from Glad to come down on a silver cloud and humor us. No, we are each our own Good Humor Man, each our own Grin Reaper. Laughter and celebration need no justification—the FUNdamentalist creed is "revel without a cause!" Master laughter—right here and right now—and you will be the object of everyone's happiness envy.

Swami Answers all Your Questions About FUNdamentalism and Nonjudgment Day.

Dear Swami:
  You're always talking about humoring other people. Suppose we don't want to be subjected to humor, but are assaulted by it anyway. What can be done?
                                    Myra Lidgen,
                                    Oak Park, Illinois

Dear Myra:
  Ah, yes. Medical people call that the Involuntary Gag Response. Humor at inappropriate times can have anything but a positive effect. Fortunately, something can be done. I was enjoying a quiet meal at a fancy restaurant when a man at the next table began joking. When he didn't stop after five minutes, I performed the Heimlich maneuver on him. Saved his life and my dinner. Since that time, I always sit in the Nonjoking Section of restaurants.

★

Dear Swami:
What do you think of Rajneesh?

Phil Spectrum,
Eugene, Oregon

Dear Phil:
Rajneesh is wonderful! I smoke it all the time.

★

Dear Swami:
My friend and I are having a bit of a disagreement. Both of us have received letters from Oral Roberts saying that if he doesn't receive a certain amount of money he's going to "go north." My friend laughed it off and bought himself a "Send Oral To Heaven in '87" bumper sticker. But I believe that if we satisfy his request it will help the progress of our souls. What do you think?

Abie Leaver,
Omaha, Nebraska

Dear Abie:
I'm with your friend. If you want to achieve enlightenment, you can't afford to get stuck on Oral gratification.

★

Dear Swami:
Can you explain the metaphysical term "transmute"?
Les Knott,
Tucson, Arizona

Dear Les:
Certainly. A transmute is someone who channels Harpo Marx.

★

Dear Swami:
  Do you accept love offerings?

                              Lois Price,
                              San Diego, California

Dear Lois:
  Actually, I prefer money, especially since I got married. As far as I'm concerned, God can take all the credit. I'll take the cash.

★

Dear Swami:
  There's someone who owes me money, but who doesn't seem in the least bit interested in paying me. I'd like to handle it in an enlightened, new age kind of way. What do you suggest?

                              Aretha Flowers,
                              Boulder, Colorado

Dear Aretha:
  I suggest that you call my friend, Swami Vitoananda, who owns a karmic debt collection agency in Chicago. First, he gently inquires about their intention to pay. If they don't send a payment in two weeks, he calls again and shares his feelings about responsibility and integrity. If they still don't pay, he comes over and breaks their aura.

★

Dear Swami:
  How many yogis can dance on the head of a pin?
                              Wyatt E. Duitt,
                              Parkersburg, W. Virginia

Dear Wyatt:
  Not many. Yogis are notoriously poor dancers.

★

Dear Swami:

*Can God make a stone so heavy that He cannot lift it?
Also, if a tree falls in the forest and no one is there to hear it,
does it make a sound?*

Loren Norder,
Chicago, Illinois

Dear Loren:

I don't know about either of those, but here's something
that's been puzzling me recently: You know the football
player Refrigerator Perry? When Refrigerator Perry closes
his mouth, does his inner light go out?

☆

EPILOGUE:

Swami Speaks out on Sects

SHOULD SWAMIS HAVE SECTS? Are we kept apart by our urges to have sects, or can sects be a way for us to express who we truly are? Will there be sects after enlightenment? In this penetrating interview, Swami tells you everything you always wanted to know about sects.

US: *Swami, let's get right down to it. What is your position on sects?*

SWAMI: You see? That is just the problem. Everyone is so hung up on positions! People always want their sects to be on top and the other sects on the bottom. So I suggest we forget about positions. Let's go for sects equality.

US: *Well, what I mean is, how do you feel about sects?*

SWAMI: You know, some people say we are all one anyway, so why do we need sects? Why make sects distinctions? It is true, we are the same regardless of our sects, but the differences are what make life interesting. Could you imagine a world without sects? It would be boring indeed. So I'm totally in favor of sects. In fact, I personally have sects in every town I visit.

US: *Some spiritual leaders would disagree with you. For example, Rev. U. R. "Tim" Tayshin of the Mortal Majority says he finds sects disgusting.*

SWAMI: Oh, without a doubt sects can appear disgusting, as anyone who's ever watched two dogmas go at it can testify. And I agree that sects without love can never bring real pleasure. But sects need not mean struggle and conflict. Sects can be really beautiful when people appreciate their differences. So let us not get sects mixed up with *sectsism*. It is not right when people believe their sects to be superior. We need better sects education to teach people to love and respect members of the opposite sects.

US: *One of our major concerns about sects is that powerful gurus or organizations will force people into sects against their will. What do you think about that issue?*

SWAMI: Oh, no. This is very bad. People should only enter into sects voluntarily. Sects can only work between consenting adults.

US: *Well then, what shall we tell our children? Do you believe there can be "safe sects"?*

SWAMI: I think we worry too much about our children because of our own fearful and negative experiences with sects. Sure, there have been a few sects crimes—and oughtism is one of the most virulent diseases on the planet, and we all know it is transmitted through sects. But why should that give sects a bad name? Let's face it, as soon as kids are old enough to walk around the corner, they are going to learn about sects anyway. So by all means, we should alert them about the dangers in certain kinds of sects. And we should teach them about safe sects—you know, don't let anyone talk you into sects, and always wear a protective shield of white light to protect yourself from oughtism. But we should also remind them that sects can be a great way for people to come together—and it can be a heck of a lot of fun, too.

US: *Do you think people should be able to change their sects?*

SWAMI: Certainly! I myself started as a Methodist, but very early on I became fascinated with the opposite sects. In high school, they called me a sects deviate because I used to dress in the clothing of the opposite sects—you know, I would wear turbans and dhotis and saffron robes. Finally, I realized I would never find the kind of sects that turned me on in Oklahoma, so I moved to New York to put my sects change into operation.

US: *Tell me, Swami, what do you think about recreational sects?*

SWAMI: I think it's a great idea. In fact, I just heard about a new church called Our Lady of the Slopes, where the entire service is held as the congregation skis down a mountain.

US: *One last question. Is there any general advice you'd like to give our readers about sects?*

SWAMI: Yes. Remember, it is a natural thing for people to have sects. So there is no need to feel guilty. And don't worry about the Second Coming. Don't worry about anybody coming. Just enjoy the moment right now, and be sure to love everyone regardless of sects.

Appendix

Editor's Note: Shortly before this book went to press, its appendix was removed. Since the appendix is a repository for toxins, you will be happy to know that this book is now completely detoxified.